BEYOND VISION

THE STORY OF A
BLIND ROWER

D0681586

BEYOND VISION

THE STORY OF A
BLIND ROWER

VICTORIA NOLAN

IGUANA

Publisher: Greg Ioannou
Editor: Kate Unrau
Front cover image: Jacqueline Schifano
Front cover design: Kate Unrau
Book layout design: Meghan Behse

Library and Archives Canada Cataloguing in Publication

Nolan, Victoria, 1975-, author
        Beyond vision : the story of a blind rower / Victoria Nolan.

Issued in print, electronic and audio formats.
ISBN 978-1-77180-027-3 (pbk.).--ISBN 978-1-77180-028-0 (epub).--
ISBN 978-1-77180-029-7 (kindle).--ISBN 978-1-77180-030-3 (pdf).--
ISBN 978-1-77180-031-0 (audiobook)

        1. Nolan, Victoria, 1975-. 2. People with visual disabilities--
Ontario--Toronto--Biography. 3. Rowers--Ontario--Toronto--
Biography. 4. Special education educators--Ontario--Toronto--
Biography. 5. Sports for people with visual disabilities--Canada.
I. Title.

GV790.92.N65A3 2014   797.12'3092   C2013-908526-2
                                                   C2013-908527-0
                                                   C2013-908528-9

This is an original print edition of *Beyond Vision: The Story of a Blind Rower*.

This book is dedicated to Eamonn,

without whom none of this would have been possible.

And to Tarabh and Ceili, my strength and motivation.

You are only as strong as the people you live with.

CHAPTER 1

The call is urgent and abrupt: "Let it run!" It is our coxswain, Laura. We stop instantly. We are carrying a $30,000 racing shell on our shoulders, and this is the A Final of the World Rowing Championships in Karapiro, New Zealand. Any damage to our boat now could cost us a medal.

We are forced to wait as the German Team cuts in front of us with their boat and gets in line for the dock. My heart is pounding. At this level, even getting to the dock is a competition, and we always want the edge. Our coach, Jeff, thinks fast and talks to an official, and we are given the go-ahead to use another dock.

I am forcing myself to take deep breaths to slow my heart down. Under Laura's direction we weave our way through people, boat stretchers, oars, and tents. Laura and I have been on the national team for four years together, so she knows how much direction I need. I have only a sliver of sight left, and getting me through this minefield of obstacles, particularly while we are under so much stress, is no easy feat. But as always, she guides us safely onto the dock.

"Ready... Up!" We throw the boat up high above our heads, and I feel around with my toe for the edge of the dock. The only thing keeping me somewhat calm is the fact that I've gone through these motions thousands of times. We lower the boat into the water, and the splash of the contact brings my focus to the conditions. We've already been told there will be a headwind, so the race will be a long one. I can hear the waves splashing against the boat and the dock, and I try to visualize what it will feel like to race in this.

Jeff gets my oar for me and places it in the oarlock. I am relieved to have one less thing to worry about. To a typical rower, putting the oar in is not a big deal, but for me, the simplest task can jack up the stress levels. I lean across the boat, feel around for the oarlock, and fasten the clip. Someone hands me my water bottle and my visor — more relief.

I hear a voice beside me. "Can I see your visor, please?"

It must be one of the FISA officials. The International Federation of Rowing (FISA) must ensure every visually impaired athlete is wearing a visor that completely blocks out all vision. Competitors are not even allowed to see cracks of daylight through the visor; even that small difference would be an advantage. Pitch-black eliminates any sense of balance.

He puts the visor on. "Oh yes," he chuckles in a German accent. "It is totally black!"

I take the visor and stand waiting for the next direction. I shake my legs to get some of the tension out.

"One foot in... and down!" That's our cue to climb in and get ready to shove off. I step onto the deck — the bottom of the boat is too thin to support any weight — and sit down. I slide my feet into the shoes that are attached to the hull and fasten the Velcro straps. I pull the visor over my head, and I am in the dark.

There was a time when this would have caused feelings of panic and dread, but I'm used to it now. I can hear Laura making her way down the boat. She stops next to each of my teammates for a handshake, a fist bump, or an exchange of some kind. Somehow she knows how to rally us together and help us focus on what we are about to do. She grabs my hand, and before she can say anything, I squeeze her hand

"Long and strong," I tell her. That's how we plan to win this race. She squeezes back. It's time to go.

CHAPTER 2

I was sitting in the dark. A single blinding light glared in my right eye. My mom was sitting in a chair behind me. It had been her idea to come here. I guess she was right — what had happened the week before proved that something was wrong with me. But I'd had regular eye checkups for the last 18 years. The doctors had prescribed glasses for me, but none of them had ever found anything unusual.

This was a new doctor. He was very curt and didn't say much to us. He was using the light to look at the back of my eye, the retina. He switched the light to the other eye, looked, and then snapped the light off. He turned the overhead lights on, but the sharp glaring in my eyes had exhausted all my perception, and I couldn't see much of anything. I blinked repeatedly, trying to see his expression. He turned to my mom and told her that I have an eye disease called "RP." He said that there was no cure and there was nothing we could do. He was so matter-of-fact and flippant about it that I shrugged it off; it seemed to be no big deal. My mom asked if we could get another opinion. The doctor seemed to take offence at this and said we could, but that anyone else would tell us the same thing. My mom seemed to be taking everything in, but she wasn't really reacting to the news yet either.

What had happened last week that brought us to the eye doctor? My family had gone together to an outdoor concert. We arrived in the evening when it was still light out and sat at the top of a set of bleachers. The concert went pretty late, and it was dark as we got up to leave. I had been sitting at the end of the aisle, and I started to step out onto the ramp beside our seats when my mom grabbed my arm. There was no ramp there. It was at least a ten-foot drop to the ground, and if she hadn't stopped me from stepping out, I'd have suffered a serious fall.

We drove home from the eye doctor without saying much. I asked my mom if we were going to get another opinion. The answer was yes.

We arrived home and found my dad in the kitchen. My mom told him the news, and he looked like he had been punched in the stomach. I didn't get it. Nothing had changed, but now we had a name for my problems. The doctor had been so nonchalant, and he said there was nothing we could do, so it sounded to me like this wasn't an issue worth discussing.

What that doctor should have told me, what I know now, is that RP is the acronym for retinitis pigmentosa, the eye disease that progressively kills vision receptor cells in the retina. It erases the world around you a little bit at a time. The decay is too small to really notice at first, but it's enough to confuse your sense of reality. RP preys on your vision slowly and relentlessly until eventually you are left with nothing.

My dad booked the appointment for a second opinion; it would be nearly six months before we could see another doctor.

The next ophthalmologist was at the hospital across the street from the first. I wondered how two doctors, in the same field, could work so close to each other and be so different. This doctor was much more informative and supportive, but the information was grim: he told me that this eye disease would gradually take away my peripheral vision. He wanted to do a test to see how much I had lost already.

He had a black board with a large white dot in the centre, and he picked up a wooden pointer, like the ones teachers use. I stared at the dot while he moved the pointer slowly around the board. I had to tell him when I could see it move. Several seconds passed before I noticed the pointer moving. He tried again in another area of the board, and again it took a while before I could see the movement. Based on these tests, he determined that I had lost a significant amount of sight, so much that I should not be driving a car. That was frightening; I had already passed the visual test for my beginners' permit, and I'd been taking driving lessons for a couple of months! I realized that this was going to be a bigger issue than I had thought.

He referred me for more accurate testing to find the exact measurement of my vision loss to find out if I was legally blind by definition. This status is qualified by a certain percentage of vision loss. My dad asked what the future of this disease would be like. The doctor said he expected me to have "some vision" for "several decades." I knew that didn't sound good.

I had another long wait until I could see the next doctor, Dr. Heon, a specialist in retinal disease. In the meantime I did some research. I learned that people have about 200 degrees of vision. Practically speaking, this means that if you hold your arms out to the sides and wiggle your fingers you can see them move — that is the extent of your visual field. Someone is considered legally blind if he or she has 20 degrees of vision or less. If you were to move your arms slowly toward the front of your body with a field of vision that narrow, you wouldn't be able to see your fingers moving until they were directly in front of you — it is one-tenth the normal visual field.

I was quietly hoping that I would be diagnosed as legally blind. This may sound bizarre, but to try to understand it, you need to know what life was like for me as a child.

I grew up with a very dark, nagging feeling, even into adulthood. I could not articulate it, but now I recognize that when I looked at myself from the outside, what I saw didn't feel like me. And the frustrating part was that I didn't know why I felt that way or how to change it. I was so timid and quiet, but I didn't want to be. There was another person trying to break free, but I held that part back and I was frustrated by my inability to let it go.

Looking back now, I recognize that my insecurity stemmed from not being able to see what was going on around me. I couldn't read people's expressions or body language, and I probably had an unconscious awareness that something was not right with me.

When you can't judge what's going on around you — the atmosphere of a room, the vibe of a discussion, body language, facial expressions — you become very guarded in your own behaviour. I have the world's best poker face; I only wish I could see the cards.

Sports were another issue. I seemed to be naturally athletic, but I just couldn't play team sports no matter how hard I tried. I remember gym classes vividly. Volleyball games were the worst. Once when the ball came my way, I was unsure what to do, so I left it for someone else. No one responded and the ball hit the ground.

"What's wrong with you? That was your ball! Next time run for it!" one of my teammates yelled. His face was red. Why was he so angry? It was so humiliating and beyond frustrating. I knew I had better run and get it next time. When the ball came my way again, I ran to where I thought it was headed and got ready to bump it, but instead I slammed into the same guy.

7

"You're an idiot!" he muttered over his shoulder. I was mortified, and the snickering came from every direction. I knew what I wanted to do, and I concentrated so hard, but it just didn't happen the way I planned.

For me, the last straw came when I was looking around trying to figure out who had the ball. It was a combination of everything at once: the similarity in colour of the volleyball to the walls and floor of the gym, my inability to track fast-moving objects, and my panic in trying not to look foolish. Of course, at the time, I wasn't aware of all of the factors. All I could think was, "Please don't let me mess up again!"

I'm sure the noise played a part, too. Isn't that how magic acts work? With a loud noise, you are temporarily blinded and unable to see the trick. Maybe the sound of the whistle or the sudden scream to "Get it!" echoing around the gym wreaked even more havoc on my vision, causing me to temporarily lose even more sight and focus. Whatever the reason, I realized I was not going to find the ball and my heart sank.

I thought it couldn't possibly get any worse. Then as I stared blankly into the open space, confused, the ball hit me on the head and bounced to the ground. Even my friends laughed, and my eyes started to sting, but I couldn't cry — that would make it even worse. The team was angry about losing: how could they know that I was losing so much more than a game? That was the last time I played a team sport. I had a million excuses to sit out of phys. ed. until I was finally able to drop the course in grade ten.

Back then I was thrilled to be rid of sports. It didn't occur to me that by not participating I was denying myself the confidence that comes from setting goals together, the thrill of achieving them, and the strength that comes from failing and getting right back up again. RP stole that from me.

There was also the issue of how people perceived me. Other students thought I was a snob. I walked right by people in the halls without acknowledging them. When I was introduced to someone and they offered me their hand, I ignored it. I walked around oblivious to what was going on around me. As a result my expression was always serious and I came across as cold. There were also mortifying moments: misunderstanding a situation, getting lost or confused, walking into things. People would laugh and ask me if I was drunk, or say things that made me feel like an idiot. When you're a teenager, everything is magnified, and the last thing you want to be is different. After having spent so much time feeling stupid and un-able, I was sure that knowing that my issues were due to a serious disability, something I couldn't control, would release that frustration. So I thought.

Dr. Heon confirmed that not only was I legally blind, but I was also functioning with only ten degrees of vision. That's one-twentieth of the typical visual field. I was stunned. Somehow I had been getting by as a "normal" person with only 5 percent of my vision! I marvelled at how that was even possible. I thought about all the things I had been doing: I was in my second year of university and doing well; I navigated busy corridors and classrooms with hundreds of people; I went to parties and dance clubs; and I read my text books... I even had a boyfriend, Eamonn, who was always supportive. Granted, I experienced many problems, but I was still doing it all. I thought I was ready for the diagnosis, but the news hit me hard.

Then Dr. Heon told me that I qualified to become a client of the Canadian National Institute for the Blind (CNIB) and that I could get a white cane. This gave me hope — if I used a cane, maybe then strangers would get it. Despite my shock at the severity of my vision loss, there were no tears, and I felt no anger or fear. There was only relief.

CHAPTER 3

We paddle away from the dock on Lake Karapiro and get lined up to enter the warm-up lanes. I can feel the energy in the air; it's electric with stress, excitement, tension, aggression. I don't have any visual distractions, but I can hear every single sound around me. Laura made sure to get us out on the water a bit early, and we start our warm-up. We have learned that we need a long warm-up to perform our best, at least 40 minutes. But the preparation is more than just physical. Really, we've spent years warming up to get where we are today. We have each fought many battles, overcome many challenges, and made many sacrifices. My life experience has prepared me for all of this; I have been dealing with the bigger challenge of going blind.

When I went to pick up my first cane, I was given a short tutorial on how to use it. I was told I could sweep the cane left to right in front of me to detect obstacles. This action is harder than it sounds, and it took some practice to get coordinated. I had to learn to swing the cane left while my right foot is forward and to swing it right when my left foot is forward. This ensures the path is clear in front of the foot that is about to step. I taught myself, using the cane in quiet situations at first. Eventually I practiced using it when I really needed it. Oddly enough, even once I figured it out, I procrastinated actually using the cane. It folded up smaller than a mini umbrella, so I carried it in my purse and pulled it out only when I couldn't do without it — if I was somewhere very dark or somewhere really busy.

I felt embarrassed using it and felt like it drew a lot of attention to me. But each time I used my cane, I was training for the day I would need it full-time. I would take a deep breath and unhook the elastic strap, and the white wand would snap open one section at a time, making a clickety-clack sound as it unfolded. It was a mental exercise for me as much as a physical one. I tried to block out the curious looks and push through my feelings of defeat.

On the positive side, it showed other people I needed some consideration, and it generally got them out of my way. For the most part, it worked: people gave me the right of way or moved more slowly. In using the cane, I realized that I had been straining my eyes to see if the path was clear and trying hard to anticipate other people's movements. With it, I started to worry less about other people, and my eyes relaxed a bit.

A cane may have solved many of my problems, but it also generated a whole batch of new ones. I could walk a bit faster than usual and it gave me a bit more confidence, but my success depended on other people's awareness of me. I quickly learned that many people walk around oblivious to their surroundings.

Learning to walk through Union Station in Toronto was the World Cup of travelling blind. It is crowded there, everyone is in a hurry, and people are seldom paying attention to what's around them. The station is brightly lit, but it doesn't matter because the sea of dark figures blocks any view of what's around. The ticket booth is in the back corner, so it's possible to walk in that general direction and scan the area for the metal posts that hold up the ropes guiding the lineup. Finding the entrance to that maze is another story, but at least if I'm in the vicinity, I can usually count on someone in line to call out and guide me where to go.

Crossing the station is more difficult. There is no flow pattern like there is in rowing. It's a free-for-all with figures moving in different directions — some going at a 90-degree angle to the right to exit the station, and some coming in; some going at a 45-degree angle toward the VIA rail station, some going at 180 degrees to the GO Trains, and some going straight ahead to the subway. And there are seats at all angles. Figures appear and disappear in the blink of an eye.

When I was first learning to navigate with the cane, Union Station sent my anxiety through the roof. The noise there was not helpful either; hearing the bustle of the people, various announcements over the speakers, and buskers only confused me more. Walking through made me feel the way I had as a teenager jumping off a cliff into the water below. I wasn't really sure if it was safe or what would happen on the way down, but I took a deep breath and went ahead anyway. If I made it to the other side, it was a major victory.

One night I was on my way home and I was crossing through the busy concourse. I drew deep breaths and used the vision I had to scan about a metre ahead, looking for people who might decide to cross in front of me. I assumed that people would leave at least that much space before cutting in front. My pace was tentative, and I cautiously made my way in the direction of the subway. Out of nowhere, like a ghost appearing, a dark shape materialized centimetres in front of me. I closed my eyes, waiting for impact. Instead, my cane was wrenched out of my hands. I opened my eyes and scanned the floor to figure out what had happened. My cane was gone, and I was able to see a man in a suit getting to his feet. He must have tripped over my cane.

My first thought was that I had failed. Horrified, I felt around on the ground for my cane and managed to locate it a few steps away. The toppled man hurried to his feet and was gone without a word. In fact, no one said a word to me. I had no sense of how the incident was perceived, whether it was my fault or his, whether people felt bad for me or thought I was a freak. I don't know which would be worse. Could I have done something differently? Or is it other people who need to change? It's such an odd place to be: neither fully sighted nor fully blind. I didn't want to be pitied, and I didn't want to stand out. I just wanted to blend in. Alone and mortified, I swept my way across the finish line and out of the building.

Apparently, so I've been told, people eyed me suspiciously and stared at me when I used the cane. It's so hard when you look as though you can see; some people accused me of faking it. I could feel the stares, and the ease I had temporarily felt while using the cane was replaced by self-consciousness and anxiety. It really is a privilege to be able to get on a bus and be anonymous.

While this entire discovery was going on, I completed my Specialist degree in Cognitive Science, and I managed to do so without assistance. Thankfully I was still able to read at that point, although I was much slower than my classmates. Looking back, I know I would have done better with some support. I did well on written assignments but bombed multiple-choice tests and computer programming assignments. I'm sure I was missing small details that went unnoticed outside of my tiny tunnel of sight.

I was hoping to continue my studies in a prestigious University of Toronto program at the Institute of Child Study. It offered a Master of Arts degree along with a teaching certificate. In 1997, I was accepted to the two-year program, and as in my undergraduate degree, my vision did not interfere in a serious way with my studies or my practice teaching.

Internationally acclaimed, the Institute of Child Study was a fascinating educational facility. I realized that this was where I wanted my career to lead. I couldn't think of anything more fulfilling than being able to teach children in an innovative, ground-breaking program. At the same time, teachers conducted research about the latest theories on education and taught post-graduate students as well. The possibilities filled me with excitement and gave me purpose. I was determined that I would make my mark in education and do something great, something that might earn me international recognition.

Eamonn graduated from Teachers' College two years ahead of me, and in 1998, while I was finishing my second year of the Master's program, we got married. These should have been happy times, but my vision was getting worse, slowly but noticeably, and my will to push through the hard stuff was weakening. As certain tasks became a hassle, I made up excuses to stop doing them. If I needed clothes, I might get ready to go to the mall, but then I'd stand at the door and debate with myself about whether I really needed to go out. I would eventually conclude that I had enough clothes and didn't need to go shopping.

One day I was running late for school and rushing to catch the bus. I was on a quiet sidewalk, so I was not using my cane. If I missed my bus, I would have to wait 20 minutes for the next one, and then I would be really late. I knew if I cut across a patch of grass I could catch it. I crossed the street and started to jog across the uneven grass. It dipped down for a few steps and then back up again. I picked up speed as I jogged downhill, and I held the quick pace as I ran up the other side. A searing pain caught me across the bridge of my nose, and I was thrown backward to the ground. I sat up and tried to gain focus to figure out what had happened. I saw a large yellow plastic tube. Guy wires cut across the grass on a diagonal slope, anchoring the nearby hydro pole. I had run straight into the wire cable, and it had cut across the bridge of my nose. I could feel blood running down my cheek. It was a 15-minute walk home, or I could keep walking and catch the next bus. I looked at the blood on my hand and felt the throbbing in my nose. I decided to go home. No one else was there, and I couldn't really see the damage to my nose other than the fact that there was quite a bit of blood. I iced it and missed school that day.

When Eamonn got home, he told me I probably should have gone to the hospital to get a stitch. After a lot of talking and tears, Eamonn convinced me that I had to stop acting as though I could see. I needed to slow down and use my cane more. I didn't want to admit it, but deep down I knew he was right. I half-heartedly agreed to use my cane more and to slow down. That choice minimized my physical injuries, but my confidence took a beating.

Things really took a turn during a trip to visit my parents in Pickering. I took this trip by myself every couple of weeks and had travelled this route many, many times. As usual, I was taking the GO Train, and I bought my ticket and put it in my pocket. On the GO Train you don't have to show your ticket when you get on, but periodically an inspector will come around to examine it. The train pulled out of the station, and I instinctively checked my pocket for the ticket in case someone came to check. It wasn't there. I searched my other pockets, but I couldn't find it anywhere. It was rare that someone came around checking tickets, but I still didn't like riding without one.

The 30-minute ride was uneventful, and soon we pulled out of Rouge Hill, one station before Pickering. With the vision I had, I could still see things out the window. We were chugging along past Lake Ontario. I always loved looking at water; it brought calm over me. There were some kayakers in a bay gliding along the water. I was mesmerized by how beautiful the boats looked, so graceful and swift. I imagined the freedom of moving that quickly with nothing around me but open water.

I was jolted out of my daydream by the sliding door screeching open. The inspector stepped through from the car behind and was coming to check tickets. I searched again and still couldn't find mine. The inspector asked me to describe the man who sold me the ticket at Union Station. I described the heavy-set man with grey hair and glasses, and she radioed my description in to the station to see if I had left my ticket at the wicket.

A message came back that there was no person by that description employed there. I was horrified. The inspector wrote up a ticket for $150. Worse than getting a ticket was the realization that my vision was so bad; I couldn't even give an accurate description of a person. I felt like I was living in some kind of made-up world, creating images that didn't exist. It was terrifying — this realization was far worse than any ticket or offence.

When I got to my parents' house and explained what had happened, my mom went straight to my coat and looked through the pockets. She pulled out my GO Train ticket. It had been there all along. This was just more evidence that I had a more serious problem than I was letting on. That was the last time I took the GO Train, and it was the day I gave up a lot of my independence. From then on, if I had to go to Pickering, Eamonn would rent a car and drive me there. I was forced to accept that I couldn't do everything on my own.

But now on the race course, it's all me. As we start to pick up the pace and practice some strokes at racing speed, I fight the urge to ease off. I can still remember when I was new at this; I would panic and think I had to conserve energy for the race, so I would back away from the work. As in life, so much of this race is mental toughness; it's so easy to give in to the pain and the fatigue. For a while I gave in to RP, and I never want to be in that place again.

CHAPTER 4

We are going through the familiar routine of the warm-up. We
have performed this sequence so many times that we don't really
have to think about it. Everything is memorized, every inch
calculated. But at the same time, you have to be adaptable. You
may think everything is on track, but you never know what's
down the course.

Despite the setbacks in my freedom, my career was going well; I
had been hired as a grade-two teacher. I was thrilled to have my
own class and to start implementing some of the philosophies I
had learned at the Institute.

I could see my student's faces, I could read their writing, and
I could read books to them, including chapter books, despite
their tiny fonts. I could write on the board and on chart paper. I
could make posters and artwork to decorate the classroom. At
the time, I didn't appreciate how lucky I was to be able to do

those things, nor did I recognize that one day — sooner than I expected — I would no longer be able to.

I set up the classroom in a way that maximized my ability to monitor what was going on. My gym classes were extremely structured to maximize safety. They involved a lot of individual drills rather than games. Perhaps it was not only a concern for safety that influenced me, but also the memories of the horrible games that I had endured in school. I was even able to teach a dance club after school for the senior students. It felt great to be able to dance again. I had plenty of space, and since I was creating the steps, I didn't have to struggle with trying to follow someone. No one taught me how to accommodate; I simply did what I had to do to succeed. Giving up was never an option. Just find a way.

Throughout that time, I was conscious of my status as a probationary teacher, and I wanted to be assessed without bias. I did not use my cane around the school. I knew I couldn't legally be dismissed from any job because of my blindness, but I wanted to avoid any possible perception that a teacher with a disability was somehow incapable.

One day, I was getting on the streetcar to go home. It was getting dark, and the forecasted blizzard was starting. I showed my CNIB pass that allows blind people to travel on public transit for free. The driver confiscated my pass, claiming it had expired, and ordered me off the streetcar. The pass was valid until the end of the month, but back then I had no confidence to argue with authority. I never spoke up for myself, so I did what I was told and got off the streetcar. I stumbled around in the snow in a completely unfamiliar neighbourhood. Eventually I found a bank machine and paid the fare on the next streetcar to get home. After reflecting on the situation, I realized that the driver probably assumed I was abusing the pass because it looked like I could see. I was beginning to feel it would be easier to be completely blind.

I started to go out only when it was absolutely necessary. I wouldn't meet friends unless someone I really trusted was there to help me, and the list of trusted friends was very short. My friend Ann Alchin was always amazing at guiding me and keeping me informed about what was going on around me, even in dance clubs! You'd be surprised how hard it is to find someone who can make you feel at ease when you're basically blindfolded. My other friends, and even my sister, Lesley, meant well, but they just didn't provide enough feedback to make me feel comfortable. I continued to feel that if I didn't have to be somewhere, why would I put myself through that situation? It wasn't worth it. I convinced myself that the groceries could wait until Eamonn came home. I could just work out in my living room.

I got a new job teaching Special Education, which meant I had smaller classes and a smaller volume of written work to look at. This move happened only by chance: the Special Ed. job was the only one available, but it turned out to be very helpful for me as my sight worsened. Four years went by...

Eamonn and I had been married for four years, and we were talking about having children. My ophthalmologist cautioned me that my vision might deteriorate more rapidly with pregnancy. This was never an issue for me. I knew I would be a great mom, and I knew Eamonn would be a great dad. If my vision worsened, then that was what was meant to happen. Eventually I was going to lose my sight completely anyway, and there was always the chance that it wouldn't get worse; they didn't know for sure. Our only real concern was whether our child would inherit this disease, but we found out that my case was not hereditary.

Tarabh (an Irish name pronounced Tar-ov) was born in 2003. The pregnancy and delivery were problem-free, and he was a healthy, happy baby. It was clear, however, that I had suffered more vision loss.

His birth coincided with the end of my ability to read novel-sized font. As a teacher I was really interested in the Harry Potter series and had read the first four books. I was eager to read the fifth, and I had preordered it to be delivered the day it was released. Tarabh was only two months old. On many occasions I tried to read my new book, but it was such a struggle that I quickly gave up each time. At the time, I figured I was just an exhausted new mom and simply too busy. In actuality, I had lost my ability to read type that size. It took such effort to strain my eyes to read each word that I not only got tired, but I also got bored because it took so long to read a sentence. That was the last time I tried to read a novel.

Making sure Tarabh is in my sight

Looking after Tarabh was manageable. I had the same stress as any new mother, and vision-related issues were generally solvable. We were renting an apartment that had lots of natural light, and it was attached to a shopping mall. It was very easy for me to get around the quiet, familiar mall. All the sight that I had left was directed at Tarabh all of the time.

When Tarabh was a year old, we started talking about having another child. This time we thought a little bit more about further vision loss.

My doctor reminded me, "If you get pregnant again, you could lose more. You could go completely blind. There just hasn't been enough research done on RP to be able to predict with certainty."

I thought about my future. I had only 5 percent of my sight anyway, and the prognosis was eventual blindness. I thought of Tarabh's future, too — how great it would be for him to grow up with a little brother or sister running around. I didn't want to control things with my vision, and I knew I couldn't. I wanted another child; if that meant going completely blind, then that was meant to be.

When I found out I was pregnant again, I was thrilled. I found the little outfit Tarabh had worn home from the hospital and laid it out on the dining room table with a note for Eamonn that said, "Here we go again!" We both laughed and were excited to find out if we would have a little girl or boy.

I planned to stay home with the kids until they were both in school full-time. My mom had done that for us, and I felt it was the best way to raise children. I didn't agree with having someone else raise my children at such a young age. Once they were both in school, I would return to my career and my teaching goals. I couldn't see everything around me, but our future looked bright.

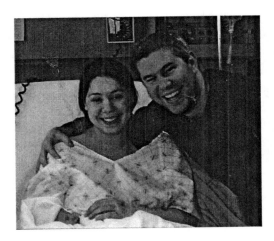

A little sister for Tarabh

Ceili (Kay-lee) was born in February of 2005, another beautiful, healthy, sweet-tempered baby. But my vision suffered, and this time it had a huge impact on me. I had now lost about 97 percent of my sight — I had lost only a few degrees with the second pregnancy, but when you have less than ten degrees to begin with, the difference is drastic. And now there were two babies to look after.

CHAPTER 5

We have had a great warm-up, the boat feels solid, and we've had enough time to go over everything until we were satisfied that everyone was on the same page. Even though everyone is nervous, we can also feel that everyone is charged up and ready to attack this race. It's time to head up to the start gates; we should have to sit for only three or four minutes before we go — perfect.

Laura lines us up perfectly in the lane; we barely have to touch it up, which is the rowing term for the gentle strokes that adjust alignment. As the official grabs the end of the boat, we hear an announcement: "Ten minutes."

You can feel the panic set in along the boat. We're not supposed to sit more than a few minutes, or the effects of the warm-up are wasted. At least all of the other boats are sitting ready as well. There was a delay in the race before us, so everything has been pushed back. We prepared so carefully, but no amount of planning could have readied us for that.

◈ ◈

Once we had kids, we decided to buy a house. It seemed like the sensible thing to do; I didn't realize how huge a transition it would be to get used to new surroundings again. We bought an older, smaller home than what we had been renting, and it was darker, too. It was frustrating, not being in familiar surroundings. I had known the old place so well that I could navigate it with my eyes closed. With the sliver of sight I had left, I knew it would be a long time before the number of bumps and bruises would decrease.

I could not manage as I had when there was just one child. Two were overwhelming. I couldn't keep both Tarabh and Ceili in my narrow field of vision, even when we were all in the same small room. I injured myself often, and I felt scared a lot of the time. My number one concern was their safety, so I was overly cautious and protective. Emotionally, I couldn't deal with the idea of them getting hurt on my watch. Even though it could happen to any parent, I knew I would blame my vision loss. It's true for both children: the only times they ever got hurt were when Eamonn was looking after them. I'm proud of myself for my vigilant parenting, but it was unbelievably exhausting to stay on top of everything. It felt like too much.

I was also housebound. I could not find a way to travel with the kids where I felt that we were all safe. A double stroller could not be pulled behind me the way I'd manoeuvred the single stroller, and I was not confident with a wagon — what if Tarabh decided to hop out and run? I reached out to various agencies for help, but nothing was available. In each case, either we earned too much money to qualify for assistance or there were no services offered. One organization told me I would just have to stay in the house until my children were old enough to walk. I was furious; I don't know how anyone could think that was a reasonable solution.

One day I'd had enough. I tried to take the kids to the park in the double stroller anyway. We had to get out of the house, and it was a short walk. I knew the route, and there were traffic lights to cross the street.

We were nearly there when I realized Tarabh was no longer wearing his hat. I hadn't noticed him throw it out of the stroller, and we had to retrace our steps to find it. It was March, and it was cold, so going without a hat was not an option. For me, it was like looking for a needle in a haystack. It took a really long time to find it, but luckily the vibrant red contrasted with the white sidewalk. I almost turned back at that point, but I was determined to get them to the park.

We reached the traffic lights. After a few seconds of scanning the air, I found the signal, and it said to walk. As we stepped into the road, the signal changed to the orange flashing stop hand, so I hurried across. At the other side of the street, the stroller stopped short and jabbed me under the ribs. It startled me, and I looked around to figure out what had happened. The stroller wheel was stuck in some leftover packed snow near the curb. I tried to tip the carriage back to get it out, but I couldn't tell what the situation was or how to fix it. It wouldn't move.

The light turned green and a truck driver stepped on the gas and squealed to a stop right beside us. The driver leaned on his horn. "What's wrong with you?" he screamed. "You've got kids with you, you stupid b——!" he snarled.

Even if I'd had something to say, I didn't have a chance. He swerved around us and was gone.

I walked to the front of the stroller and heaved the whole thing onto the sidewalk. I told myself that it was not my fault and that the guy was just crazy. But part of me thought he was right: I shouldn't be out with my kids.

The entrance to the park was just across the street, and Tarabh was already calling out "Park! Park!" I fought back the tears and pushed on.

Thankfully Ceili was fast asleep, snuggled in her blanket. I unclipped Tarabh's seat belt, and he was off. I was shaking from what had just happened, and all I wanted was to collapse on a bench. Being the overly cautious mom, however, I followed Tarabh around trying to make sure he was safe.

Tarabh was having the time of his life as I struggled to keep him within my sight. He whipped around the playground. I dodged monkey bars, swings, and poles, but the inevitable eventually happened: I smacked my head on a low-hanging post. That was the last straw at the park. With my son in tears, I packed everyone up and we headed back home.

I couldn't fight against this disease anymore; it had taken control of my life. I spent day after day cooped up in the house worrying about what I wasn't doing for my kids. I was miserable.

Then I faced a reality I had not even considered.

Eamonn pointed out that if I went back to work my days would be easier. Even though I would have more children to look after, I would have more support and more structure. I was devastated. I wanted to be home with my own kids until they started school. I didn't want them to be raised by strangers. But I knew he was right. I realized, sadly, that even though they wouldn't be with me, I would be a happier person, and they would be able to go out and do the things other kids do.

I tried to look at it as a glimmer of hope. Okay, maybe we had to change the plan a little, but I didn't have to give in to RP. I could still pursue my teaching goals and accomplish things despite this disease.

I planned my return to work, and about a month before I was due to go back I met with my principal to let her know about the changes in my vision. We concluded that with some minor accommodations I would be able to return to my job.

In the meantime, I tried to enjoy my last month at home with Tarabh and Ceili. One day we were eating lunch when the doorbell rang. I opened the door and someone handed me a registered letter. I signed for it, wondering what this could be about. I tried to read the return address, but the sunlight was too bright. When I brought it inside, I recognized the logo in the corner. It was from the School Board.

As I strained to read the letter, one phrase stood out: until I met with a Board physician, they considered me unfit to return to work. A million things flashed through my mind. My biggest concern was, of course, Were they going to fire me? I was also baffled as to why my principal would have initiated this without telling me. It was like a slap in the face, and I felt betrayed.

That was only the beginning. The hope of returning to work, to an environment of support, acceptance, and encouragement, was now filled with suspicion, belittlement, and barriers. My principal questioned the severity of my vision loss; she questioned my ability to teach; and she denied me positions based purely on her assumptions about what I was and wasn't able to do. She told me that parents would not support me as a teacher, and she tried to persuade me to quit teaching.

I would not quit. Teaching was my dream, and I had left my children for this, I was not going to give up on it easily. The principal would not give me a classroom; instead, she assigned me a program that did not involve teaching curriculum. The students in my classroom needed to be supervised the way Tarabh and Ceili did. I had to make sure they didn't run out of the classroom or do anything dangerous, and my students were unable to talk. Can you imagine a worse placement for someone with vision loss? It was as though she was setting me up for failure.

It was a struggle to get up each day. I couldn't bear to think that this was my future — feeling distant from my children, feeling like I was a disappointment, not being able to do things with them. Then I had to face going to work each day surrounded by people who were doing what I had always dreamed of but now wasn't allowed to do. It wasn't because I wasn't able, but because I was being denied the opportunity.

While other teachers helped their students write letters to children in other countries, or read novels to the class, I followed my students around to stop them from eating chalk or climbing on shelves. When I wasn't stressed about their behaviour, I was frustrated trying to teach them colours and numbers for hours, day after day, with little progress. My spirits sank lower and lower as the days went by. My self-esteem was gone. My confidence was gone. It got to the point that I couldn't muster enough courage to leave the house. RP had finally won; I was ready to surrender.

There is a theory in the psychology of racing that if you advance on your competitor in a race, you only have to do it three times to break them. People have the mental strength to hold you off twice, but the third time you push back, they will fold. RP took away my mobility, but I pushed back. It took away my ability to parent my children, but I fought back. When it took away my career, it broke me.

Things were bad for a year and a half. In retrospect, that doesn't sound that long, but living through it was an eternity. When you let your challenges govern your life, you lose your self-esteem and you lose your purpose in life. The days were endless, and I felt lost. I am so thankful that Eamonn and the kids were relentless in their support. It was Eamonn's philosophy and the inspiration of Tarabh and Ceili that pulled me out of that darkness and into a light I had never even dreamed of.

CHAPTER 6

"Seven minutes."

We can't change the time of the race, but we can try to stay warm. Laura asks the official if we can do a start sequence and then row back up. It's allowed. We sit ready, and Laura calls a start.

I can only imagine how distracting and confusing this is to the other boats as we take off from the start pontoon, but it's exactly what we need.

Laura aggressively calls for speed. All the other boats just sit there, probably wishing they were us but afraid to move. Our hearts are pumping again, blood is flowing, and we have a psychological advantage over everyone. We row back up to the start with two minutes remaining until the race begins. It couldn't have been more perfect.

Sometimes, what seems like a negative situation can be turned into a positive just by thinking about it differently.

◈ ◈

I was suffering because my career in teaching wasn't panning out as I had planned. The one thing I was passionate about had been taken from me. But Eamonn kept planting this seed: what if I found something else to be passionate about? I resisted the idea for a long time; teaching was all I had ever wanted to do. But I was also thinking about Tarabh and Ceili and how I appeared to them. I did not want them growing up thinking their mom was limited. I knew that as they got older they would have to deal with having a blind mom, and I wanted to turn it into something they could be proud of, not embarrassed by. Reluctantly, I heeded Eamonn's advice. What did I have to lose?

I wanted to find something I could do independently. Then, even though the kids had a blind mom, they could say, "Yeah, she's blind, but she can ——." I just didn't know yet what that might be.

I decided that whatever it was should be something that would get me back in shape. Although I spent adulthood avoiding team sports, I had always been interested in getting in shape through solo athletics like aerobics, dance classes, or even running when my sight had been better. Between the pregnancies and not leaving the house for a couple of years, fitness was definitely a good choice.

I started joining my friends in their assorted athletic pursuits — rock climbing, salsa dancing, fitness classes — but there were many barriers, sometimes even before I got to the class. One by one, I crossed each activity off my list of potential passions.

In January 2006, Brian McKeever, a visually impaired cross-country skier, won two gold medals for Canada at the Paralympics in Torino. My good friend Ann emailed me the news article with a message: "Hey, Vicky, I think you're slacking off!"

She was only joking, but it got me thinking. There were all kinds of sports out there for blind and visually impaired athletes, and I should check them out.

The Canadian National Institute for the Blind really encourages sailing. It is supposedly empowering to be able to control a vehicle independently, particularly because a blind person lacks the opportunity to drive a car. I found this idea intriguing, but I wanted something that was more of an aerobic workout.

With boats in mind, I thought about other water sports and wondered what rowing was like. I didn't know anything about the sport. I had never even seen anyone row, but I loved being on water, and rowing definitely involves aerobic endurance. I wondered if anyone in Toronto even offered rowing. I did a quick search online and found The Argonaut Rowing Club.

When I went to their homepage, I was surprised to discover that they had a "Learn to Row" course for people with physical disabilities! I was so excited to attend something where I knew I would be welcome and where I could succeed.

The staff there told me that I should be able to take the regular Learn to Row course and that I didn't need to be in the adaptive class. This was fine with me! They understood my disability, and they knew which program was best for me. It was also great news because it meant I could join with one of my friends. I had a really hard time finding anyone who was willing to join. Everyone said it sounded like too much work! Finally my friend Nade agreed, and we signed up.

In rowing, a racing shell is very different from a canoe or a kayak. It is a very long, narrow rowing boat designed for speed. Rowers propel the boat with long oars and the power of their legs, and the seats slide forward and back to allow for maximum power. The design of the shell makes it very unstable, and it must be actively balanced, or "set," to avoid flipping.

On the first day of the course, I realized that I had no idea what this sport was all about or anything about how to do it! This became apparent right away as we watched a safety video. The narrator explained how to put your feet into the shoes that were part of the boat — they were strapping their feet in! It seemed a little frightening. What happened if the boat tipped? But before we had time to discuss it, the same video showed us what "catching a crab" is all about.

Catching a crab is the rower's biggest fear; it haunts me at every competition. It usually happens because you are gripping your oar too tightly. The oar enters the water at an angle instead of dropping straight in. As the boat moves forward, the oar gets pulled down and under, and the pressure of the water is too great to pull the oar back out. By the time you wrench the oar free and start rowing again, catching a crab can add seconds to a race time. There's also the potential for injury if the handle of the oar catapults back into your body or face.

In the safety video, the rower's oar got sucked under water and twisted around, then the rower was launched into the air by his twisted oar. It was as if someone had hit an eject button. Nade and I looked at each other in horror. The instructors assured us that ejection from the boat never happens. I still felt uneasy and wondered what I was getting myself into.

We were told that we would be taking out an eight, which is a shell with eight seats. The boat was almost 20 metres long and weighed a little over 90 kilograms. We were expected to lift the boat off the racks in the boat bay and carry it down to the water.

The instructors decided that someone would carry the boat down for me and bring me my oar, and then I could get in the boat. This was great news. All the equipment, instructions, and potential tripping hazards were overwhelming to me, and I was relieved to have assistance.

Each rower had one oar, and mine was on the right side of the boat, or the port side. I was also told that I was in the "six seat" and would be referred to that way during the practice. At the back end of the boat was a tiny seat for the coxswain. This position is essentially a coach in the boat. Coxswains are set up with a headset, and there are speakers throughout the boat. They make technical calls for the crew and steer the boat.

We pushed off from the dock. We started rowing in pairs; the first two seats went first with constant direction from our coxie. She moved through each pair of seats, and after some manoeuvring and lots of reminders about which side was port and which was starboard, it was my turn to row.

My blade splashed into the water, and my legs drove my seat backward as I pulled my oar in toward my body. I popped the oar out of the water and slid my seat forward, preparing to take another stroke. Again I pushed with my legs and pulled with my arms. This time I pulled a little harder. As we got going, we tried rowing in fours. The boat surged through the water. Stroke after stroke, I loved the sound of the oar hitting the surface of the lake and the gurgle of the water running under the boat. I loved feeling the speed we were moving at; the land in the background appeared to be whizzing by us. Most of all, I loved that I was making this boat move.

It was sloppy at the beginning; the boat bounced from side to side, and I sometimes missed the water as I tried to place the oar, but it was such an incredible rush. It was so liberating, and I felt so safe — no risk of being hit with a ball or bumping into anyone.

When the session ended, I couldn't wait for the next class. That's how quickly I fell in love with this sport.

CHAPTER 7

"One minute!" A voice rings out over the loudspeaker.

The officials are starting the lane poll, calling each crew to ensure they are ready to race. This is it. My arms start shaking uncontrollably.

"Ireland…"

I take a deep breath. I have a heightened awareness of all the sounds around me, but I try to ignore them and focus on my goals for this race: at each 250-metre marker, I am going to take my effort up a level, and when it hurts, I am going to pull harder. There is no crowd at the start line; they are all at the finish in the grandstand, but the noise from the six boats is overwhelming. Two lanes over, I can hear someone vomiting over the side of the boat — a common reaction to the nerves and anticipation of the pain to follow. I force myself to breathe and mentally rehearse the start sequence.

"Germany… Great Britain…"

I know they are beside us. I can feel the tension. I can hear all the coxswains directing their crews. The different accents, different terminology, it all blends together into garbled voices, and I try to block that out as well.

"Canada..." Tony, a teammate, gives a cheer from the back of our boat, but I'm so nervous that even his enthusiasm is a distraction. Meghan, in the seat behind me, pats my back, and we sit up in position. I slide my seat as far forward as I can, pulling it to my heels. My upper body is turned to the right, so my oar is reaching back as far as it can be. I sit up tall and try to have a light grip on the oar as I wait for the last few calls.

"Ukraine... United States of America... Attention..."

Laura tells us to bury the blade, which means making sure that it is under the surface of the water. This ensures the strongest connection.

"Red light... Attention..."

"Red light" is the verbal cue given for the visually impaired athletes. Once the red light comes on, the race is about to start.

I know that once the call to row is given, I will be fine. It's the anticipation that is hardest. I am solely focused on hearing that word, making sure my feet are ready to dig in the instant I hear it. I don't hear any other sounds now — that's how focused I am. It's only 4 seconds from the word "attention" to the word "row," but it feels like minutes. My legs are restless, and my arms have not stopped shaking. I know if we can just get going, I will be fine. I know we can do this. I want to go!

"Row!"

I take the first stroke sitting strong and tall, making sure the blade of my oar is buried just under the water. My feet are connected, and I pull the handle to the right height on my ribs. All of a sudden the boat dips slightly and my blade loses its connection. For a split second I panic, but I quickly get the oar back to the correct height and put extra jump into the next stroke. I finish the start sequence strong, and I can feel that we are solid and all on the same page: the boat is set, and there is a strong, solid rhythm to the stroke. The run on the boat is smooth, and we are fast! A rocky start, but we got it back.

My Learn to Row course did not start smoothly either. The instructors were concerned with my progress over the next few classes. Apparently I was not keeping time with the other rowers. The reason was clear: I couldn't see what they were doing. At first the instructors weren't sure what to do, and that could have been the end of team rowing right there. But they found a way, and it was quite simple: from now on, I would be in the "stroke" seat (the seat at the front). I would be the one who set the rhythm and timing, and everyone else would have to follow me.

This is a perfect example of how people with disabilities can easily be included. All it takes is a little bit of thought and creativity, and maybe a little adaptation. Instead of having a knee-jerk reaction — "he can't" or "she won't be able to" — we should strive for inclusion: "how do we find a way?"

Once I learned the technique, I was able to row in any seat, and I could follow the rhythm by feel.

The start sequence was good, and the race is going well. I've already forgotten about the stroke I missed. We're winding up the speed now, ten hard strokes on the legs. My quads are already on fire, and we're not even through a quarter of the race. I'm hanging on the oar, feeling the pull through the lateral muscles in my back with every stroke, accelerating that handle through to my body. We are flying!

Laura's voice comes over the speaker "Okay, here's the story: we're in third place. Great Britain is out, Germany is moving, and we've got to go!"

"No way," I think. "We are not getting third." With that, my competitiveness squashes the pain. I sit taller and pull harder. "If it hurts," I tell myself, "it's working." I'm not letting them have an inch. I want to win.

For 30 years I lived a life without competition. I'd never had a taste of it, so I didn't know what I was missing. And I just wasn't the athletic type — or so I had thought.

On the last weekend of the Learn to Row course, I was standing on the dock holding my cane, waiting while the boat was carried back to the boathouse. Some of the club rowers were on the dock getting ready to go out.

There was a very friendly man on the dock who seemed to know everyone. He was over six feet tall, and even with my loss of vision I could see that he was muscular, likely an elite athlete. It wasn't until he moved across the dock with a limp that I noticed one of his legs was a prosthesis. He approached my friend and me and introduced himself as a competitive rower on a team for people with disabilities.

His name was Wilfredo Moré Wilson, but everyone called him Papito. He told me that he rowed on the National Team and that he had won a bronze medal for Canada. He was hoping to make Canada's first Paralympic rowing team and compete in the Beijing Games. This was my first exposure to Paralympic Sport.

Papito also told me that I would qualify for "Adaptive Rowing" (for rowers with physical disabilities). In order to compete in adaptive rowing, a person needs to have lost a certain amount of sight or mobility. Papito inferred from my cane use that I had lost enough sight to qualify, and he encouraged me to give competitive rowing a try.

I explained that I had no desire to row competitively. I had never been competitive in my life. He was persistent. He introduced me to Allison, the coach of the Argonauts Adaptive Team, adding with a big smile, "You never know. You might go to Beijing."

I laughed. He had no idea how athletic I was, but he had convinced me to give it a try.

The team trained every Tuesday and Thursday night for two hours. The club was not easily accessible by public transit. This meant not only would Eamonn need to get me to the club after work and wait around for two hours to drive me back home, but he would also have to look after the kids for those four hours a week. It really didn't make sense for me to go through all that hassle when I could just row for fun when it fit into our schedule. But without hesitation Eamonn agreed to take me, so it looked like I was going competitive.

That Tuesday I met the group; they had quite a range of abilities. James and Linda were a couple in their fifties who were recently married. James was visually impaired, and Linda had an eye disease that also caused hearing loss. Linda was a former veterinarian and professor from the United States. Mitzi was a young woman whose leg had been amputated after a motorcycle accident. She wore a prosthetic leg. Juan and Bill had each had a leg amputated, and both used crutches. Bill had had his leg amputated to stop bone cancer. He cracked jokes constantly and was always so positive. It was a great group of people to be around. Erica, a high school student, had cerebral palsy. Of course, Papito was there, too, and also Alyssa Vito, an able-bodied rower who rowed for Michigan University on a scholarship. She was a remarkable person who volunteered countless hours of her time to cox and coach these athletes despite having an extremely busy schedule of her own — including an hour's commute home! I also met Allison, the head coach who organized the boating arrangements and competitions. I found out she was also the coordinator for the National Adaptive Rowing Team.

As everyone started to get organized, I watched four of the athletes carry a shell by themselves, directed by Alyssa. James and Linda were in the front, and Erica and Bill were in the back. Bill balanced the boat on one shoulder and used his crutch on the other side as he hopped across the dock.

I stood there with my mouth open in disbelief. There would be no princess treatment with other people carrying things for you here. This was a tough sport, and I needed to get my act together. This thought thrilled me.

Sometimes I trained with Mitzi, sometimes Erica, and sometimes Juan. It was hard work, especially with only two people in the boat; it took a lot of effort to move it. I got raw spots on my hands from gripping the oars and sometimes got what are known as "slide bites," bruises and marks on my legs from hitting the slides of the boat that hold the seat. But I loved it. The fact that you had to be tough and push through pain made me love it even more. When a headwind blew up and the boat felt really heavy, I would grit my teeth and pull harder. Each person I rowed with told me how strong I was, and their encouragement made me even more determined.

I overheard conversations about what rates the able-bodied rowers competed at, and I started trying to hit those targets myself. I even bought myself an erg (short for ergometer, which is an indoor rowing machine) so that I could practice even when I couldn't get on the water.

My first race was the Dominion Day Regatta on Toronto Island, on Canada Day in 2006, and we entered a women's coxed four with Linda, Erica, Mitzi, and me in the boat. We had never rowed together, but I was excited to be in my first race. Maybe we would even win it! I had no information about who was competing or how many entries there were, but I was full of excitement.

When I arrived Allison gave me my racing uniform to change into. I held it up to look at it, and I was horrified. The unisuit was basically a bathing suit — a spandex tank top attached to spandex shorts. It was striped horizontally with light blue and dark blue stripes. I didn't want to go out in public in it! I didn't feel like I was in shape at all, and I still hadn't lost the weight I'd gained from being pregnant. I pulled on a pair of capri pants over the unisuit to hide the extra weight until race time. When I finally had to take the capris off, I held my breath, trying to look slightly slimmer, but I knew it wasn't doing anything! Besides, holding my breath wouldn't change the shape of my arms!

As we warmed up, I learned that there were no other rowers with disabilities in this race; we would be racing able-bodied rowers. I was surprised. There was no way we could compete with them.

We lined up at the starting station, and before I knew what was happening, the official called "Attention... Row!" and we were into the race.

Our start was not in sync at all; the boat was flopping from side to side. I missed a couple of strokes as I panicked and tried to go too fast. A crew has to practice together to know how to move quickly together. We had not learned that lesson. I could hear Eamonn at the side cheering us on. I couldn't tell where the other boats were in relation to ours, so I just kept pulling, but I was tired and I could feel my energy fading. I threw my body behind the oar as I pulled. The whole thing was frantic and I was exhausted.

We finished dead last, far behind any of the other boats. I was surprised and not sure what had just happened. The loss did not sit well with me at all. If I were going to do this, I would want to win. I wanted to get faster and beat those able-bodied athletes! And so it started — I realized that competition was in my blood.

The kids were too young to really know what had happened. Eamonn was telling them to congratulate me, so for all they knew, I had done well. My team was content with the result. They had been through this before and were happy just to participate. Participation was okay, but I wanted more.

I increased my training, determined to get fitter and stronger. I was out on the water every chance I got, and I worked out on the erg a few times each week.

In August there was a provincial regatta, the Ontario Championships. There were two boats entered for the Adaptive Mixed Four — two men and two women per crew, all of whom had physical disabilities. My boat came in first, and we won the gold medal. Even though there were only two boats in the race, it felt amazing! It was the first medal I had ever won in my 31 years on the planet, and I did it blind.

My children were thrilled. I put the medal around Tarabh's neck and he showed it off proudly.

Sharing my medal with Tarabh

I continued rowing in different combinations — pairs, fours, eights — and many of the people I rowed with encouraged me to try out for the National Team. That's what Papito had talked to me about earlier that summer.

After the Ontario Championships, I was invited to join a crew that was going to compete at the Royal Canadian Henley Regatta. This was one of the biggest regattas in North America and took place in St. Catharines during the second week of August.

I was going to row with James, Juan, and Erica, and we were going to race against the National Adaptive Team's mixed four. This would be the boat I would be trying out for, if I decided to go that route.

I was really excited; this would be a good race! It was also a chance to see how good I really was. Our crew was able to practice together twice before the regatta. I had high hopes of coming close to the National Team's time. That shows how little I knew about high-performance sports!

The night before the race, all the adaptive athletes met at a restaurant for dinner. I arrived late and joined the table of about 20 people. I was seated at the opposite end of the table from the National Team four, and I sat with some of the single and double rowers. I couldn't tell who among them were coaches and who were athletes, but everyone there impressed me. Even though there were athletes who would be competing against each other, the atmosphere was supportive and upbeat. Everyone was excited and chatting about their training and other competitions. Some of them were studying law or finishing university; one man owned a fitness studio and consulting business. It was a group of people who were confident, successful, and driven to excel.

As we left the table, the image really struck me: about half the athletes were in wheelchairs; some grabbed crutches; others, I noticed, had cerebral palsy or vision loss. I would never have known any of them had disabilities. I felt a sense of excitement — I wasn't sure why. Maybe it was a sense of belonging. This is where I fit in.

The race was over before it began. The National Team blew us away off the start and beat us by a lot. But that didn't deter me from wanting to be on the team; in fact, it was more of a challenge thrown down. Now I had something to prove.

We continued practicing for the last month of the season.

My first Henley competition:
Juan, me, Papito, Erica's mom, and Erica (in front)

One evening I was rowing in a four and Alyssa was coxing us. Out of the blue, Linda told Alyssa that I was going to try out for the National Team — which I had not officially said I was planning to do.

Alyssa said, "Good. I think you have a really good shot." Her opinion meant a lot to me, and it was the push I needed to actually commit to trying out. I decided there and then.

When I told Eamonn, he put a little more fire underneath me. He thought that I would do really well because he remembered when we used to run together. He had always been impressed with how I pushed myself to keep going long after he was done, and as the workout went on, I pushed harder. He said I was like a machine. That phrase stood out for me. I had never thought of myself that way — but I trusted him. Despite my excitement, deep down I didn't feel like I was good enough to make the team, but I concluded that if I tried out, at least I would have an inspiring story to tell Tarabh and Ceili.

I continued rowing through the winter. I had to get on the erg every day. I imagined trying out for the National Team and being able to go to China to compete. My visualization grew to the point where I imagined bringing my mom, who had always wanted to go to China. I dreamed that I would be the one to get her there. It was a fantasy, but it pushed me through some long, boring rowing sessions in our freezing-cold mud room after the kids had gone to bed.

In order to be considered for the National Team, I had to go for an erg test every two months. The test required that I race on the rowing machine for 1,000 metres and then submit my time to Rowing Canada Aviron (RCA). After five test submissions, RCA would decide if I was invited to the selection camp to make the National Team.

My first test was slow. At the time I knew nothing about race plans or what it felt like to pull a test, so I knew there was a lot of room for improvement. As I grew more familiar with the tests, I had concrete goals, numbers to aim for during my workouts. This helped to keep me focused and gave me a specific goal to work towards.

In February I competed at the Canadian Indoor Rowing Championships, a massive erg competition. Monitors were hooked up to the ergs, and each erg projected an image of a boat that moved according to how hard the rower was pulling. This way, spectators could watch a virtual race.

Getting coached by Cathy at the Indoor Erg Championship

Generally, rowers rely on the rowing machine's monitor to push themselves. The monitors display your time over 500 metres, which is called your "split." With my vision, I could not see the monitor at all, so I needed an official to stand behind me and read out the splits.

Before I started the race, I asked to be told my distance every 250 metres, and I also asked the official to tell me if I went off my goal split.

My time was 6 seconds faster than my first try. I got such a rush from concrete proof that my hard work was starting to pay off. Six seconds is a huge improvement over just a couple of months. It wasn't competitive yet, but it could only get better as I trained more. My goal for the next test was to knock off another 5 seconds. I kept training, and the scores kept getting better.

In June I got a letter inviting me to the National Adaptive Rowing Team (NART) selection camp in London, Ontario. I was thrilled. Now my kids could say, "Yeah, my mom's blind, but she was invited to try out for the National Rowing Team!" There seemed to be a pattern emerging: when I accomplished one thing, I had to go one step further. Now I didn't want to just try out, I wanted to make the team.

CHAPTER 8

In the forefront of my mind is executing the race plan: sit tall; draw in high; swing over the knees. Laura is calling for legs — stand on those foot-stops. We are still in the first half of our race, but planted deep in the back of my mind is all I've been through to get to this point. It has been a roller coaster of emotions: all of the training and sacrifices; being on the opposite side of the planet from my husband and children; and most traumatic of all, having my guide dog Vegas taken away from me. Vegas was denied entry to New Zealand, taken from me at the airport, and shipped back to Toronto. When it happened, I was so helpless. All I could think was that I had to win a medal to make this all worthwhile.

I draw all those emotions into pure power, and it's as if I'm beginning a whole new race. I am surprised at the strength that comes. My lungs ache and my legs feel like they are disconnected from the rest of my body, but I've entered a whole new commitment in this race — I cannot back away from the pain. I pull harder.

◈ ◈

To understand how much my guide dog fuelled my desire to win, you need to understand the bond that a handler and a guide dog have. I didn't grow up with dogs, and initially I did not want a guide dog. Finally, I gave in because it was a way to deal with my decreasing mobility.

Typically, when a person is placed with a dog, he or she is expected to live at the guide dog school for one month with no visitors to be trained in how to use the dog properly. This was not an option for me at the time. I did not want to be away from my family for any length of time.

When I found out about Fidelco Guide Dog School in Connecticut, getting a dog became a possibility. One feature that makes them stand out is their "In Community" placements. Fidelco trainers will go to a client's home and work with them in their own community. This was exactly what I needed, so I applied.

The application itself was quite involved, which is as it should be. A doctor's referral must be provided, as well as character references, and a video depicting the prospective handler's mobility skills. Applicants must also participate in an interview. A few months after all of that, I was told I had been approved. I spent a couple more months on a waiting list, but before long I met Jason Stankoski, a professional guide dog trainer, and with him my new guide dog, Jetta.

Jetta was a black-and-tan German shepherd. She was small for a shepherd, only about 60 pounds. Having never had a dog before, I was nervous and awkward interacting with her. I had a lot to learn, but I had a friend for life. Little did I know that her time with me would end sooner than I thought.

There are very specific placement and training routines for new guide dogs. My first day with Jetta was spent bonding. Wherever I went in the house, I had to keep her with me at all times. She had to remain on a leash, but I did not discipline her at all. I gave her lots of love and rewards, and I was the only one who was supposed to feed her. This ensured she would know that I was the most important person in her life. Jason also told me that I should feed my family before feeding Jetta so she would understand her place in our "pack." At night she slept on a mat beside our bed.

After the bonding period, Jason returned to teach me how to travel with Jetta. There was a series of voice and hand commands that I needed to learn to communicate with her.

The first day, I stood with her on my left side and held the harness in my left hand. The harness not only identified her as a service dog but also allowed me to feel Jetta's subtle movements as she walked. The basic commands were "forward," as the right arm extends straight in front; "halt"; "left," as the right hand sweeps left; and "right," as the right hand sweeps right. The guide dog relies on your body position and gestures in addition to the verbal cues.

We practiced these in front of the house until Jason felt satisfied that we were ready to try walking around the block. Then I held the harness, raised my right arm parallel to the ground, and said, "Jetta, forward."

Jetta started walking, and I followed her. Her pace was surprisingly quick, and I had to adjust how I was used to walking. She moved more quickly than I was used to travelling, but I had been instructed to go with her and let her guide me. People with dogs can walk faster than those with canes. She stopped and indicated that we were at the end of the sidewalk — this was amazing! I signalled for her to turn left, and she steered me gently around to the next stretch of sidewalk.

This stretch was considerably longer than the first. Again, I matched Jetta's pace. The street was busy with cars whizzing by beside me, but Jetta did not waver in her path. She was focused and steady, leading me confidently down the sidewalk. I held my breath as I saw the shapes of people approaching. It's really hard to put your trust in an animal, and I wondered what was going to happen as we got closer to the other walkers.

Jetta smoothly guided me in a wide path around them and resumed her straight course. More people approached, and I felt the tension in my shoulders again then suddenly realized I didn't need to be afraid. I was beginning to trust my dog. Memories of more independent days came back — I used to always walk this fast! — and a rush of excitement came over me. I walked with my head held high for the first time in years. At the most insecure time in my life, Jetta brought me a feeling of security.

We continued to train. Each day we walked for hours, dealing with every possible obstacle or scenario you could imagine — garbage cans in the middle of the sidewalk, construction, other dogs, cars. Jetta passed all the tests. She was so intelligent, constantly looking ahead to anticipate what she needed to do to keep me safe.

Oddly, Jetta seemed to consistently get confused turning left. Jason couldn't figure out what was causing the trouble because she did everything else perfectly. When her turns didn't improve, Jason decided to take her back to Fidelco for a month for a little bit more training.

When Jason and Jetta returned, we resumed training and Jetta was great. I learned how to travel on the subway and on buses. Jetta was trained to bring me onto the vehicle, and with the command "find a seat," she brought me to the nearest available seat and put her nose on it! I couldn't believe she was doing this for me and didn't understand why. She was a beautiful, amazing creature.

She even took me through the dreaded Toronto Eaton Centre without any problems during the busy holiday shopping season. Smoothly and gracefully, we weaved in and out of crowds, and boy, did people get out of my way when they saw a German shepherd headed toward them! A trip like that used to cause me so much anxiety, but with Jetta by my side I had no need to worry.

Jason told me about the laws pertaining to service animals. They are permitted anywhere that people go, and we had no problems taking Jetta wherever we went during training. Jason said he had noticed Canadians seem more aware of these laws than Americans are.

Our training concluded, and Jason left. I continued to get to know Jetta, and I got more accustomed to using her. I took a night school course and was able to handle the 30-minute walk home in the dark confidently, not only because of my ability to navigate with Jetta but also because I knew that no one would confront me while I had a German shepherd by my side!

I began to notice that Jetta had some anxiety at night; she tended to growl at people and was suspicious of them. Jason had explained that nighttime made some dogs nervous because their vision was compromised in the dark. I knew how they felt.

Jetta's anxiety went a little deeper than most dogs, as was discovered on a follow-up visit by another Fidelco instructor. The instructor stopped by to see how things were going after three months and observed us in action in order to assess how Jetta was doing. She followed us as we travelled and watched us get on a subway.

I was shocked to learn what Jetta was doing on subways. Whenever we got on, I asked her to find a seat, and we always got the seat right by the door. I had assumed we were just lucky that the seat was always open. But apparently Jetta would walk over to the person sitting there, stare at him, and bare her teeth slightly. The person would move, and I would sit down. Without realizing what had really happened, I would pat her on the head and tell her she was a "good girl"!

The Fidelco instructor concluded that Jetta was too skittish and too aggressive to remain as a guide dog. She took Jetta away that night and retired her from guide dog work.

I had mixed feelings about this. I was angry and frustrated that it didn't work out after I had finally accepted the fact that I needed a guide dog. But I also knew that it was for the best, and I knew that Fidelco would find me a better dog. As amazing as these dogs are, they are not perfect, and there can be some trial and error involved in finding the right match. In August 2007, I got the call that they had a new dog for me.

Fidelco made the right match with my next partner; Angus was an excellent guide and gorgeous in every sense of the word. My image of him is like a lion: regal, proud, and loyal. While Jetta gave me the confidence to get back up, Angus brought me strength and courage to start fighting against going blind.

I don't think I'll ever have another dog quite like Angus. He was a German shepherd like Jetta, but he was long-haired and very dark compared to her. He had long tufts of hair under each ear that felt like velvet when you stroked them, and he was extremely handsome and distinguished looking. One woman told me that he had Richard Gere eyes, and another said he was like Sean Connery! Angus loved to be with the family and sat with us wherever we were. He loved to be on the couch watching TV with us. I'm pretty sure he thought he was human.

Training went well, and I picked up right where I'd left off. Angus was a good guide and had no problems turning left. Jason told me that every dog has his "thing," and Angus's was that he lost control when he saw another dog or a baby. Either would make him bark until he was corrected to stop with a quick tug on his collar.

On the last night of our training, Jason, Angus, and I walked through a busy neighbourhood. We had been all over the city, tried every type of transportation, and encountered countless obstacles, and Angus had mastered it all. We were practicing night travel, the situation where Angus and I felt most nervous. Angus was much more comfortable at night than Jetta had been, but nighttime was when I had the least amount of sight, and I think he sensed my uneasiness.

We walked for about two hours along busy streets and quiet streets, and in and out of stores. With every step, the bond between us grew. He was amazing: the way he kept checking behind to be sure I would clear an obstacle; the way he slowed his pace to indicate a narrow path; and the way he weaved his way gracefully around people who blocked our path. Angus passed all the tests, and my confidence was growing. Jason was really happy with our progress, and we decided to call it a night.

We had already walked so much that we decided to take a taxi home. Typically in Toronto, there are taxis everywhere. Whenever you decide you want one, you can raise your arm and expect to be on your way somewhere in a cab within minutes. Even with my limited vision, I was able to hail taxis, but I had no idea how much that was about to change.

Jason hailed a cab, and I heard it pull up. Jason opened the door and started to get in, but he stopped. I heard the driver's voice from inside saying, "I don't take dogs."

"It's okay," Jason explained, "it's a guide dog."

"I don't take dogs!" the driver said more loudly.

Despite Jason's efforts to explain the law, the driver absolutely refused to take me. Jason recorded all the driver's information; the driver actually gave him a business card and wrote his name on it. As the cab drove away, Jason held out the card to me.

"You can't see this," he laughed, "but on the corner of the business card there's an accessibility symbol. So much for that!" We filed a complaint with the City of Toronto. Then I had to wait for a court date.

Jason told me that this rarely happened, but as I would discover, it happened more often than he thought. As it occurred more frequently, a battle started raging within me: part of me wanted to avoid conflict and felt extremely reluctant to use Angus, and the other part of me was determined to educate people and change things. But Angus was my partner in this, quietly leading me to make a difference, giving me the strength to start becoming the person I always should have been, and it made our bond so much stronger.

CHAPTER 9

"Heads in, this is our race. We're moving on Germany. That's it, it's working! You know how to move this boat. Great Britain's in first. We're moving into second. We need more power on the legs, on this stroke. GO!"

One of the roles of the coxswain is to motivate the crew and distract them from the unbelievable pain of being in the race. Rowers train their minds to ignore the signals of distress that the body sends out during a race — these are signals that the body naturally pushes you to listen to. Despite all the training, the temptation to ease off is always there. For example, if you are not getting enough oxygen to the lungs, the body's natural alarm system thinks you might be dying. Every fibre of your body might be screaming for you to stop, but in a race you have to find a way to keep going. One of the worst things you can do is look out at the other boats; you need to keep your focus inside.

In this way, the blackout goggles I have to wear actually help me. I can't see anything, not even a crack of light. I have no visual distractions, so I can be inside my head, focused on Laura's voice and concentrating fully on feeling and hearing the rhythm of my teammates. It took a long time for me to accept those blackout goggles and see them as any sort of asset, but I've learned how to use them to my advantage.

About a week after I was invited to the NART selection camp, I got a casual email: "By the way, you will need to get yourself a pair of blackout goggles, as all visually impaired rowers are required to row with them."

My stomach dropped. That sounded terrifying! At the time, I couldn't understand why anyone would force someone to be more blind than they already are. Blackout goggles are basically a pair of ski goggles with the lenses painted black so that no light can get in. The point was to create an even playing field so that all visually impaired athletes had the same amount of vision. The thought of having no vision at all made my knees weak, and I was tempted to back out, but something told me I was strong enough to take on that challenge.

The camp would be six days long, and it was held in London, Ontario, about two hours from Toronto. This would be the longest I had ever been away from the kids, and I was so worried about how they would handle it. Ceili was only two — how could I leave her without a mom for a week? I felt like I was abandoning them. Eamonn assured me that it was healthy for them and healthy for me. I felt incredibly guilty, but I tried to convince myself it would be good in the long run, that it would fix the way I had been feeling. I hoped it would improve how I felt about myself, and how Tarabh and Ceili viewed me in the future. With a tearful goodbye, I took a deep breath and tapped my way in to the University of Western residence with my cane.

The residence was actually nicer than what I remembered seeing when I was at school. We were staying in units that had individual bedrooms with a shared a kitchen and bathroom. The rooms were modern and bright. I was sharing a kitchen with Meghan Montgomery, who had been on the team for a year. Meghan hadn't arrived yet, so I decided to wander around to see if I could meet some of the other athletes. This wasn't like me, but I felt some excitement and confidence in knowing that I was there as part of a group of people my age who also had disabilities. We shared an understanding that wasn't always possible with able-bodied people.

As I went out, the door across the hall opened and a woman introduced herself to me; Laura Comeau was trying out for the coxswain position. Of course, that meant we were trying for the same boat because the other boat classes (the mixed double and the men's and women's single) do not have coxies. Laura did not have a disability, but because the coxswain position is more of a coaching position rather than a physical one, the athlete filling that role can be able-bodied.

Laura had been coxing for ten years — since she was in grade nine! She had wanted to row, but because she was small and light, she was asked to cox instead. Laura was now one of the top coxies in Canada, and she had been asked by Al Morrow, the coach of the National Women's Team, to consider this position to broaden her experience.

The coxie is basically a coach in the boat. Although she is responsible for steering the boat and keeping a straight course, her most important job is coaching the rowers to maximize their effectiveness and increase their speed. A coxie also becomes a sort of personal trainer as they try to motivate you to pull harder and not think about the ever-increasing pain that is creeping up on you.

Laura and I headed outside to find the rest of the group. Everyone seemed to be arriving at the same time, and they were easy to find. My excitement was growing. I hadn't spent much time thinking about whom I would be hanging out with for the week, but as I was starting to feel like I had at that dinner in St. Catharines: I fit in here.

Meghan was from Winnipeg and had competed as an able-bodied rower until she learned there was a Paralympic rowing team. When she was born, the fingers of her right hand did not fully develop, but Meghan had never looked at herself as having a disability and had played many sports growing up. When she discovered rowing, she had expected coaches to tell her she couldn't do it and had been ready to challenge them on that. To her surprise, no one discouraged her, and she developed a hand strap similar to a weightlifting strap that helped her to grip the oar. She had been rowing for five years and, before discovering para rowing, had made the Manitoba Team for the Canada Summer Games and won bronze. In 2006, she had rowed at the World Championships on the para-rowing team and won bronze along with Tony Theriault, who was also at the NART selection camp.

Tony Theriault was an incredible athlete from Nanaimo. He had first tried rowing in high school, where he won the BC Championships in a quad. In university he started competing in triathlons and competed in the Ironman World Championships in 1991 in Hawaii. He finished with the fastest Canadian time. While training for the next World Championships, however, Tony was hit by a speeding car while out on his bike. The accident caused a spinal cord injury that damaged muscles in Tony's legs. A true athlete, Tony got right back into sports, continuing with triathlons and then rediscovering rowing. He had incredible upper body strength, and as I got to know him, I discovered he had a great attitude toward sport and competition.

Scott Rand had tried out for the boat last year, but he ended up not competing in the World Championships. He was an engineer from Calgary, and he'd had his leg amputated below the knee following an accident at work. He hadn't discovered rowing until after his accident, and he rowed wearing an amazing prosthetic leg that was designed to have a flexible ankle — apparently this was unique and rare, and it gave Scott an advantage against other rowers with prosthetic legs.

There were a few more athletes trying out for our boat, in the LTA4+ category. This is a category for athletes who have a physical disability, but LTA stands for legs, trunk, and arms, and represents what the athletes use to propel the boat. There are two other categories in terms of physical ability: TA, for athletes who have use of only their trunks and arms; and AS, for athletes who use only their arms and shoulders. Four is the number of rowers, and the plus sign indicates that there is a coxie.

The mixed double boat — mixed because there was one man and one woman — was in the TA category. Some of the athletes trying out for this boat used wheelchairs, while some, like Papito and a few athletes who had cerebral palsy, could walk. The final category was the men's single and women's single, which were in the AS category. Almost all of these athletes used wheelchairs and had little range of motion in their legs and trunks.

All of the athletes had only physical disabilities. I am clarifying that because Paralympic Sport is separate from the Special Olympics, which are for athletes who have intellectual disabilities. Often people think they are the same thing, but they are two separate events.

I learned that there would be a couple of days of training. Then we would participate in something called "seat racing" to determine who would be selected for the team.

For our boat, no other women were invited to compete for a seat, but there was one other man challenging. That meant we had to race with the different male combinations in the boat to see which pairing was fastest with Meghan and me. Once that was decided, we would have to do a time trial to see if we were fast enough for Rowing Canada to send us to the World Championships. There was also another coxie trying out, so we would have to time trial with each coxie to see who moved the boat fastest.

Just listening to these athletes and hearing their perspectives on life had already made this experience worthwhile. I had a great time at dinner getting to know everyone and hearing stories of past rowing experiences, but I was about to get a rude awakening about the real life of a competitive rower.

The schedule of a rower, relative to that of most people, can best be described as insane. A rower typically begins her day before the sun is up so that she can get on the water at first light. It is expected that a rower will be pushing off the dock at 5:15 a.m., and that's the easiest part of her day!

At this camp, we were given a break and didn't have to be up until 6:30 a.m. We stopped for breakfast on the way to Lake Fanshawe, which is located within a conservation area. When we arrived at the London Training Centre, we met Al Morrow, the coach of the Women's National Team as well as former Olympian and World Champion. He was our host for the week and was very kind and welcoming.

While we sat in the meeting room getting our information, National Team rowers were carrying oars, fixing boats, stretching, and warming up. They were extremely focused on what they were doing and did not give any indication they knew we were there. Their tall, muscular shadows were very intimidating as I watched from a distance. We met the National

Team coaches; the coach for our boat was Anne-Renée. She would provide all the workouts and coaching for our boat. She informed us that we were going to have two practices a day. I wondered if I would be able to keep up.

The first row was about an hour and a half, and by the end I was pretty tired, but it was a good workout. Then we had to carry the boat back to the boathouse, all uphill. It was tough, and I was proud of myself for doing it. I was looking forward to going back to the residence for a rest before the next row, but we had to go grocery shopping.

By the time we got to the store, fatigue had set in. My legs ached. My stomach grumbled. I had no clue what I should buy. The five of us (Laura, Meghan, Scott, Tony, and I) tried to negotiate meals to cook together. It seemed to take forever to get everything sorted. In the meantime, I was so tired I was dizzy. As we walked around the aisles I tried hard to focus my vision on an object so I could walk in a straight line. It took all my concentration just to walk! When we got back to residence, I showered and wolfed down some food. Fifteen minutes later it was time to row again.

My body was weary, and I had a hard time lifting my feet to walk. We carried the boat down to the water again and rowed long stretches of Lake Fanshawe without stopping. This row was hard on my hands; the spots that had been tender after the first row now turned into wide blisters. I was used to shorter distances and more breaks. I was obviously the newest member of the boat, and I had a hard time keeping up with everyone else, both in technique and endurance. As hard as I tried to be technically accurate, I became less and less refined as I grew more tired. I could hear the frustration in the voices of Laura and our coach, but it didn't deter me from trying. In fact it made me more determined to learn what they were telling me to do. Despite the exhaustion, I fought hard to follow their directions. I may not have had an athletic background, but I began to realize that I had something equally valuable — mental toughness. My ability to stay focused through pain and exhaustion is what kept me going. That's what Eamonn meant when he said I was a machine. I would not quit; I would only work harder.

Day after day I trudged down to the course and held it together for the duration of the practice, mentally collapsing at the end of each one and dreading that walk up the gravel path to the boathouse. Every weary step was agony, and I often had to fight back tears.

The vision-related injuries only made things that much more difficult. When we were picking the boat up out of the water we had to bend over the boat and throw it over our heads. One day I didn't notice that I was standing in a spot alongside the boat where the rigger sticks out. On a shell, instead of the oars being attached to the boat, they are attached to riggers that extend a few feet outside the boat so that longer blades can be used. For obvious reasons, this is a bad place to lift from. As we flipped the boat over, I felt a sharp pain as the rigger jabbed into my thigh. I couldn't do anything about it because we had the heavy boat on our shoulders. I was already exhausted and my leg was throbbing. A hideous bruise eventually formed; it was dark purple in the centre and was surrounded by a circle of yellow and blue. The whole thing was about the size of a fried egg. Scott started calling it "the eye of Sauron," from the *Lord of the Rings* movie. It was good we could laugh about it, because otherwise it might have been overwhelming.

Laughter became really important. As we got to know each other we would make fun of our disabilities and our quirks, but in a positive way that brought us closer together. I would ask Meghan if she needed a hand, and we would laugh. We joked about Scott needing so much time to get ready and called him "high maintenance." And we would just laugh about things in general. It made practices much more manageable.

I was nowhere near ready for the amount of physical exertion I went through in those first few days. I could never have imagined what would be expected of me, and I was not prepared, but somehow I made it through. And then we had seat racing.

CHAPTER 10

Even though my body is in distress, it's a good feeling. I know I am strong from the hours of training. This pain is different from the frustrating pain I felt when I first started training with the National Team, the pain of struggling to keep up. This is a motivating pain that tells me I am succeeding and that I have to maintain that effort. The old pain only caused panic, but this generates confidence. We are getting silver!

The seat races were tough, we were expected do five 1,000-metre races in a row, one after the other, to compare times. I was in the stroke seat, which was good on one hand — I didn't have to worry about following — but on the other hand, it was a lot of pressure because I was setting the rhythm and therefore the speed for the whole boat. It was torture: I was gasping for breath, my muscles screamed in pain; and I was trying to execute all the technical calls Laura yelled at me. When she yelled for more power, I thought my lungs were going to explode. Worst of all, the others didn't seem to be hurting the way I was. It was the worst feeling in the world to be the weakest link.

The team was selected as we had predicted: Laura, me, Meghan, Tony, and Scott. With seat racing behind us, we had a few days of practice before the moment of truth — the time trial. Now we had to prove that we were fast enough to compete with the rest of the world. The remaining days followed a similar routine of raw hands, aching muscles, difficulty breathing, and utter exhaustion. I swore that I was going to get myself in shape. I would never let myself feel this inadequate or be in this much pain ever again.

I don't know what hurt more: my muscles, the large puffy blisters on my hands, or the embarrassment. Laura and Meghan talked in hushed tones, and I knew they were venting about my weakness. That was hard to deal with. I was starting to feel like I didn't belong here; I wasn't an athlete, and if the group didn't accept me, then I was definitely not going to stick around. But at the same time, both Tony and Meghan said the boat was moving much faster than in the past and that I was strong. I was proud to play a part in increasing the speed, and I knew I had so much room to improve that it would only get better.

The team's new speed also meant we actually had a chance of being selected to go to the World Championships, and I couldn't ignore that opportunity. All of a sudden it seemed a very real possibility that I was going to row for Canada! I had sure come a long way from the trials I had faced in the past: the GO Train, the park, the cab drive, the hydro wire. And I was starting to uncover what had escaped me for so long. I was figuring out who I was.

Me, Meghan, Scott, and Tony training on Lake Fanshawe

The night before the time trial my stomach was in turmoil. I was so nervous, and I was absolutely dreading it. If we didn't make the time they were looking for, this would be the end of the road for me. I hadn't imagined I could actually make the team, but now that I had a chance, I wanted it more than anything.

I spent most of the night going over our race plan and visualizing the technical details I had to remember:

- Sit tall.

- Keep hand levels straight all the way in and out.

- Make sure the hands clear the knees before moving forward.

- Glide the slide.

I fell asleep playing it over and over in my head.

I got up at 5:00 a.m. and could barely swallow my oatmeal. It kept sticking in my throat, and my stomach was all over the place. We had to be ready to race at 7:00 a.m. Every action had to be executed at a precise time. We could not be at the start line any later than 6:55, we raced at 7:00, and the second race went off at 7:05.

Time was reported frequently to keep everyone on track. We all had specific duties to do at specific times: boat out and bolts checked at 5:50; oars down to the dock at 6:00; team meeting at 6:05; hands on the boat at 6:10; walking the boat down to the dock and pushing off by 6:20.

Everything went according to schedule, and Al directed us through the start of the trial, where he was an official. There were two official timers at the finish.

We followed our race plan. Laura timed it and thought our time was good, but the race officials would have a more precise time. Factors like wind and current would be considered in a complicated formula used to calculate a percentage. We had to make 96 percent of the world record time. Great Britain held the world record of 03:30 in a strong tailwind. Our goal was 03:40 (96 percent), and Laura thought we had pulled 03:45, but we did not have a tailwind, so our time was looking good.

There were meetings and phone calls with Rowing Canada and the Paralympic Committee. We all sat around waiting to hear the results. Eamonn and the kids arrived; I would be going home after the decision was made. After almost four hours we were finally called in to the meeting room.

Allison began the meeting by summarizing the week — things that went well overall and what needed to change. Then she described the phone calls that had gone back and forth between RCA and her. I was pretty sure our boat had made it, but I was still worried, and I really wanted the other boats to make it too. It would be horrible if she announced that only some of us would be going to the Worlds. It felt like she was dragging it out too long! Finally she announced that all of the crews had been approved. We would all be going to Germany to represent Canada at the World Rowing championships.

It was surreal; I had made a national sports team. I was going to represent Canada! I was in shock. Eamonn immediately grabbed his phone and called everyone we knew. Tarabh and Ceili were still too young to understand what was going on, but they knew I had done something to be happy about, and I knew one day this would be a big deal to them.

Before we left London, Anne-Renée brought our team together.

"We have a lot of work to do between now and Germany," she said to the five of us. She was obviously not impressed with what she had to work with. "You need to get in shape, all of you. You look like you came here thinking this would be something fun to do," she continued. "Now we are a National Team, and we need to take it more seriously. In three weeks when you come to Montreal, you had better be in better shape."

This cast a more sombre tone over the whole experience. I knew I had a hard summer ahead of me, but I still found her words motivating. This was exactly what I needed, a new passion. I may not be able to do elaborate projects with my class or engage in research, but I could certainly get on an erg or out in a boat and row.

I was determined that I would never go through this pain again, and now I also wanted to impress our coach. I had three weeks.

CHAPTER 11

We have raced 250 metres so far. The countless hours of training are definitely paying off; everything is automatic, running like clockwork. My body knows exactly what to do. As I grow tired, I tell myself to sit up; if my arms start to hurt, I push more with my legs. I have learned all these tricks from not only relentless physical training but also mental training. When I think of that first year, when I knew nothing about sports psychology or pushing limits and had very limited fitness, it's incredible to see how far I have come.

Rowing Canada paid for our team to train together for a week in Montreal. They even covered the cost my train ticket to Montreal and accommodation at McGill University.

As I prepared to go, I was a nervous wreck. This time, I would be travelling on my own, and Eamonn and the kids would be too far away to visit. I was travelling to a city I didn't know to spend a week with people I didn't really know. I was committing to train with a national team — something else I knew nothing about. And I was doing all of it without sight.

As always, Eamonn helped me to focus. He said that if I hated it and I wanted to come home, he would drive all the way to Montreal and bring me back. I laughed; it was not in my nature to quit, and we both knew I would never make that call, but it felt good to have his support and know I had options.

When the train station attendants saw me and my cane, they helped me board the train and find my seat. In fact, I seemed to get special treatment. The seats of the train were set up in pairs, and my seatmate was an older man who smelled like cigarettes and alcohol. The train started moving, and an attendant brought around newspapers. The man slurred something to her in French, and she gave him a paper. I was not looking forward to spending the whole journey beside this man. She seemed to sense my uneasiness and told me to come with her. She gave me my own two seats closer to the front of the train. As the train rumbled on, I sat looking out a giant window and was able to see beautiful green farmland all the way to Montreal. I listened to music and enjoyed the peace and quiet, not thinking about what lay ahead.

The music was all downloaded from my computer, but I discovered a song I had never heard before. It was the type of music Eamonn would listen to: punk rock mixed with Irish music. I half-listened to the words while I searched for the skip button, but the chorus stopped me in my tracks: they were singing about someone named Vicky and how she was a fighter with a warrior's soul.

I had never heard a song with my name in it before. I thought maybe Eamonn had added it to inspire me, but he can't keep a secret, so that didn't seem likely.

The song is actually saying "Micky," rather than Vicky. It's "The Warrior's Code" by the Dropkick Murphys, and it was later featured in the movie *The Fighter* about Irish-American boxer Micky Ward.

Eamonn and I still don't know how it ended up on my computer, but that day "The Warrior's Code" gave me strength, and I started to see myself as a bit of a warrior — battling my way through fear and insecurity.

I arrived in Montreal and, again, had support from the train attendants, this time finding my way out of the train station and into a taxi. I felt very fortunate; because it was so busy, I wouldn't have had a clue where to go. The taxi took me to McGill. I was the first one to arrive, so I went up to my room.

The residence was horrible! It was old, and because it was so poorly lit, I had a really hard time figuring out the layout. As my eyes adjusted, eventually I could make out the decor: various dark shades of brown blended together with little contrast. The room was just big enough to hold the two twin beds, and they were unusually low to the ground. At the foot of one of the beds was a small desk. The brown cell was cramped and dingy, and the beds were practically touching each other.

My heart sank as I thought about spending a week like this. It's one thing when you're young, but I had thought I was past the days of residences and uncomfortable sleeping situations. I was tempted to get a hotel room, but I knew that was not practical. My feelings of dread came back, and I wished I was back at home. When the others arrived, I was relieved to hear they felt the same way, but of course our only option was to deal with it; this was all Rowing Canada could afford for us.

We were completely on our own at this camp. Our coach, Anne-Renée, lived in Montreal, so she would meet us each day only for our practice. Although it was all paid for by Rowing Canada, our transportation, accommodation, and meals had to be organized and managed by us. Our residence did not have a kitchen for us to cook our own food, and it was quite a journey to the course by public transit. In some ways, solving these problems brought us together as a team, but at times it created conflict and tension because it was not easy for any of us.

We were training on a course at the Olympic Basin, which was built for the 1976 Olympics — how cool is that? If my journey with the National Team ended after Montreal, it would still be an awesome experience! To get to the course, we walked to the Metro station, travelled for half an hour on the train, and then walked another 15 minutes. This was fine for the first morning, but once the workouts started to catch up with us, the journey got more and more arduous, particularly for Scott and Tony, who did not have full use of their legs.

I thought the workouts in London had been tough, but they were nothing compared to what we did in Montreal. I had prepared myself better for this camp and felt ready to take on the kind of volume we had in London, but I quickly learned that I was not as prepared as I'd thought. We would train from 7:30 to 9:30 each morning, go for a snack, and then row again from 11:00 to 1:00. It was gruelling.

Anne-Reneé coaching me

The intensity was higher because there was no time trial at the end to save energy for. Anne-Renée's goal was to work us hard, and she certainly did. The duration of the workouts was longer, and we were focusing on speed — speed I was not used to. It was so hard to keep my technical focus when my hands had to spin so quickly. I would forget the sequence, fatigue would set in, and my body would slump down instead of sitting tall. The coach would shout for me to sit up, or to spin my hands out more quickly, but my body just felt limp and would not cooperate with me. With fatigue, even your brain starts to slow down, and I felt like I couldn't achieve what I was trying to do. Laura had told me about a hundred times to hold my knees before moving forward. I was so focused, and I was giving all I had, but I was exhausted. I knew everyone was frustrated with me, and my being the stroke added so much pressure.

The blisters I got that week were unbelievable; I thought the ones in London had been bad. Because of the humidity and the speed at which we were spinning the oars, the sores were bigger and in new places. They were always open because we practiced so often and didn't have time between rows for them to dry. They grew bigger as the days wore on. I put Band-Aids and surgical tape on them before every row, but they always fell off partway through the workout. Some of the blisters had gone so deep that they bled during practices. The pain of pushing through the workout, the burning I felt down my throat, and the fire that burned in my quad muscles and biceps all paled in comparison to the stinging, throbbing, screaming pain of those blisters. Every time I pulled on that oar, I winced in agony.

But the worst pain of all was back at the residence. After a long day in the boat and the hour-long trek back to our temporary home, I would be yearning for a hot shower to soothe my muscles. When I stepped under the hot water I would forget, for a second, about the state of my hands. As the hot water ran down my arms and over my palms, it was all I could do to stop from screaming. I cannot describe the multi-level pain — aching, stinging, sharp and throbbing all the same time. I kept my hands out of the water and used the very tips of my fingers to rub in soap or shampoo. It took forever to feel clean since I couldn't use my hands. Then I stepped out of the bathroom into the dingy room where I couldn't see, and I wished more than anything that I was home.

By the middle of the week I was so tired I could hardly swing my cane back and forth as I walked. Another song I'd heard on the train was stuck in my head; this one was by Jewel, called "Life Uncommon." The line that stuck with me is when the singer says that however tired she is feeling from fighting, she isn't worn out. I must have played that line a hundred times in my head, and each time I would take a deep breath and push on. I thought of Tarabh and Ceili one day telling their friends that their mom rowed for Canada, and it gave me strength. I was doing it for them, and I could endure anything for them. I would not cave.

The very last day of the camp we were racing against two other boats to practice our race plan. By then I was so tired and nervous that I didn't care about racing. I was missing my family, and all I could think of was going home.

To calm my nerves, I told myself that this race didn't matter, that it was only a practice. I told myself I could just go through the motions of keeping the boat in time without putting any real power into it. Why do that to myself? I could just get this thing over with and then go home. The important races would be in Germany.

We were blown away by the other two boats, and our coach was furious. She knew exactly what was going on. Mine was not the attitude of someone who was going to represent Canada. The others were worn out too, but that hadn't stopped them from going hard in the race. I knew they were frustrated with the result too. I got what Anne-Renée had been saying about a National Team attitude, but it was going to take me a while to truly learn what that meant.

I went home for three weeks before we got together again for Munich. Unfortunately this was how the program was run, with only a few weeks to train together. The rest was up to us to train individually at home. The National Adaptive Rowing Team in Canada just didn't have the money or resources to have a centralized team the way Great Britain did.

You can imagine that with my limited experience and no coach, my training situation wasn't ideal when I was home. But I followed the workouts our coach gave us as best I could. Often I couldn't get on the water at the rowing club because I didn't have someone to row with, so I would use the erg or go for a run with Eamonn instead. Sometimes I was so tired I thought it would be better to recover than to plow through the next workout. I later learned this strategy was very wrong!

Through all of my training, Angus, my new guide dog, would lie tied to a picnic table patiently waiting for me to return. He did not like to be separated from me and got nervous when I walked away from him and got on the water. I knew this because he would start with whining, and as I got farther from him, escalate to barking. He barked incessantly while I was in the boat, as if to say, "Don't go, you need me!" Whenever we rowed by him, he would whine until we were out of sight and repeat this with each lap I made of the course. Then Angus would go absolutely berserk when I returned from a workout, so happy about my return and eager to work for me again. He would whine and be frantic to get to me. As soon as he was loose, he'd scramble around his harness trying to get into it.

We had another week-long camp in London before flying to Germany. But for this camp, I was excited. My time away from home had a real purpose to it: by the end of this chunk of time away with my team, Tarabh and Ceili would finally be able to say, "Yes, my mom is blind, but she rowed for Canada in the World Rowing Championships!"

I was starting to feel improvements with my rowing, and my mental focus was getting stronger during times of fatigue. But I still felt the same frustration of being the weak link on the team.

We continued training in the days leading up to our flight. The training finally seemed a little more manageable to me; however, every time we picked up speed my technique suffered. I still had to be reminded over and over again to hold my knees down and keep my shoulders relaxed. It was like a broken record; day in and day out Anne-Renée, who we now called "A.R.," would shout the same phrase through her megaphone: "Vicky, hold your knees down!"

Meanwhile Laura's voice over the speakers would give a longer version of the same thing: "Vicky, make sure as you swing out that your hands cross the knees before you break them. If you break the knees before your hands are clear, your blade dips and then starboard can't get their oars to the water."

It was the same thing every practice. I got it. I understood it. But remembering to do it and having the strength and speed to do it while exhausted was another story.

The frustration in their voices deflated any motivation or drive I had in me, and my mindset returned to just wanting to get the practice over with. Before I went to bed each night, I wrote down the things I was working on, and I fell asleep going over them in my head.

A huge part of the learning curve was working with a sports psychologist. It was fascinating to hear how it's possible to change the way you think about things and use negative feelings to your advantage. For example, instead of giving in to the pain and thinking that you can't go on, you can think differently: the chemicals in your body that are active at that point of fatigue are bubbling up inside you as a secondary energy source. Of course, this is not actually the case, but thinking of it this way it is so empowering, and much better than feeling defeated.

So much of the fight through fatigue is mental. If you can put a positive spin on things, you can push through anything. The sports psychologist also used my experience as a mother to help me. He pointed out that I endured hours of pain in childbirth, and I did it twice. The race is over in three and a half minutes. Thinking of it that way made it seem so doable!

What helped me most that year was realizing that what makes competition enjoyable is how tough it is to win. Beating other boats without having to push very hard would never mean as much as having to fight for it and push your own personal limits. It was a revelation to me, but at the same time it seems so obvious. It's all the pain and sacrifice that make a victory so much sweeter.

Before we left for Munich, we were racing in the Royal Canadian Henley Regatta in St. Catharines. We were set to race an adaptive four from Ottawa — a similar boat to the one I was in just a year earlier. Everyone was certain we would win by a long shot and that it would be embarrassing to pick up a medal because it would be such an easy win. This assumption was because, as was my experience the year before, the team from Ottawa wouldn't have had many opportunities to train together and would not have been doing the volume that we had been doing. But this was our first official race as a crew, and we practiced as if we were going to the Worlds.

I was more nervous than usual for this race. There were the usual reasons, but this time we also had a large audience watching from the grandstands, including members of everyone's home clubs. This was added pressure I wasn't used to.

This would also be my first race with the blackout goggles. I had practiced in them, and I had grown to really hate them. It was frightening and frustrating to try to row without any visual cues whatsoever. Sometimes we would stop to talk, and I would forget whether my oar was squared in the water or feathered, and I couldn't just look at it to tell. Rowing in pure blackness made the hours drag on and on. And when we did racing pieces, trying to keep up was pure panic, feeling the speed but having no sight whatsoever. As each practice began and I put the elastic over my head, the smell of the plastic made me feel nauseated. I began to associate that smell with those feelings, so before I even began the practice, I was anxious. I had to take deep breaths to overcome the panic and anxiety it gave me.

We did our warm-up, and my nervous energy grew. I was breathing hard already, and we were just warming up. I held back, trying to save my energy for the race. It was painful to push through the warm-up, but on the other hand I wanted to warm up forever and never start the race. All of a sudden, earlier than expected, we were called to the starting gates.

I could hear the stress in Laura's voice as she tried to get our boat straight in the starting gate.

"Tony touches it up. Meghan backs it. Sit ready. Tony touches it again. Tony touches it again."

"Okay," she said, "sit ready."

We all sat with our seats pulled up to our heels, our arms reached out. My oar bobbed in the water as I held it lightly in my fingers. I was in pitch-black, taking deep breaths. We heard the official: "Attention... Row!"

Instantly we pushed our feet against our foot stretchers and pulled on the oars. It was so heavy that it felt like rowing through mud. Then we pulled quicker and quicker strokes to get moving until we got the boat up to speed. We had pulled out in front. We followed our race plan, listening to Laura. "Stay calm and do what she says," I told myself. I couldn't tell how close the race was, but I kept pulling.

At 500 metres I was dying. How could I possibly do another 500 metres? But I couldn't let this boat beat us — we were the National Team! I had to ease off because I was so tired, but I tried to keep up. Before I knew it, Laura told us it was time to sprint; we had to pick up the rate even faster. I couldn't think straight. I tried to spin my hands faster as we approached the finish. I could hear the crowds in the grandstand getting louder as we approached the finish line. My hands were cramping up from gripping the oar so tightly, and my arms were so exhausted that I forgot all about "the bubbling energy" and my hands started to slow down.

Disaster! In my state of fatigue, my mind wandered away from feeling the rhythm of the boat to just pulling hard. I thought that might make up for my slow hands. I was too tense, and my oar was not completely squared. It was sucked under, and I caught a crab. The boat jolted backwards and rocked side to side. I tried to yank the oar back out, but I was too panicked. Laura told me to stay calm, but it was taking too long for me to get it back. Normally you can pop an oar back out from catching a crab within a couple of seconds, but this was closer to 5 seconds. It felt more like 30.

When I finally got it out, I had lost the rhythm of the boat. I was in pitch-black, and I panicked again. Instead of trying to feel the rhythm, I just started rowing in my own time. This threw everyone off. Right in front of the grandstand, Scott caught a massive crab because of me, and this time we actually had to stop the boat.

We only had about 100 metres left to go in the race. Laura called for us to start again, and we rowed the last ten strokes across the finish line. I was horrified; I had caused us, the National Adaptive Team, to be beaten by a club crew. We would have no credibility now. I was mortified.

Laura directed us to row up to the podium dock, and as soon as my hand touched it, I ripped off my goggles. The crowd was applauding, but I wanted to die. Laura helped me out of the boat, and we walked toward the podium.

"What's going on?" I asked Laura. There was an awkward pause as she tried to figure out what I meant. We were being directed to the podium, so she took my arm and helped me to the centre of the dock.

We lined up and were each given a Henley medal. I figured this must be a new thing, a participation medal or something. Normally they only gave out gold.

The other boat was waiting in the water. The crew called out, "Congratulations!"

I paused and looked at Laura. "Wait — did we win?"

The team all started laughing as they watched me realize, incredulous, that we had still won the race!

"So, we have learned something today," Meghan said, putting her arm around me. "When we are in Germany, Vicky needs to know if we won or not!"

The Royal Henley experience definitely got rid of a lot of my racing jitters, but I was not proud of that medal. It was an easy win, and I backed down when the pain hit. Again, it would take years for me to fully internalize what winning really involved.

Before we left for Munich, we were given our kits. Rowing Canada provided us with the same uniforms as all the able-bodied crews going to Germany. It included pants, a jacket, T-shirt, golf shirt, and long-sleeved training shirt, shorts, and another dreaded unisuit that we would compete in. I tried everything on right away, including my racing unisuit. This unisuit was even more revealing than the Argos Club unisuit because it had solid-red shorts and a white top with a red horizontal stripe across the chest. I did not like how I looked, but I was wearing a Team Canada uniform! It didn't seem real.

We finished our last practice on Canadian water. We were drifting at the bottom of the course waiting for A.R. to come over and tell us to go in. The pieces we did were very good, and we were fast. We congratulated each other, and a wave of accomplishment and pride washed over me.

While we were waiting Laura's voice came over the speakers: "Guys, tomorrow morning we'll be in Germany!" It seemed crazy. We had to get off the water, shower and pack, and leave for the airport within the next two hours. I definitely was not used to such a fast-paced lifestyle.

As we continued to wait for A.R., Laura told us a really silly joke over the speakers. Worried we were going to get yelled at, we tried to stifle our laughter, but we couldn't stop and it echoed around the lake. It felt so good to be sharing jokes with them. As my rowing technique began to improve, I was also getting to know my team more, and I became more comfortable with them. I finally felt accepted. I was part of the team.

CHAPTER 12

"Okay, Canada, you're in second. Germany's still coming after us. GB is still out. This is our focus: get us to the 500!" For a fleeting second, I consider that silver is better than we have ever done. Silver is nothing to be ashamed of. But just as quickly, I smash that thought. That's the pain talking, and I know Germany is still coming for us.

I was really stressed about the trip — not just the travelling but also travelling with my guide dog for the first time. Even as it was happening I marvelled at how I managed to juggle so much without my head exploding. But I drew confidence and strength from the fact that I had survived all that crazy training, and I was travelling as a member of Team Canada. I felt I could handle anything.

I had planned Angus's eating and toileting very carefully: only half his dinner the night before, and just a handful of food for breakfast; limited water until close to the end of the flight; and a pack of "Wee-Wee Pads" in case of an accident.

I was so worried about how the flight staff would react to him that I kept my sunglasses on; this seemed to help people fully understand the situation. With the glasses on, however, I surrendered the last bit of sight I had left. I had no choice but to get help.

Every staff member was extremely generous and helpful. Someone walked me through security, which meant I not only had assistance putting my things through but also skipped all the lineups. Instead of feeling like I didn't belong, I was actually getting VIP treatment here.

But the biggest treat of all was on the plane. The flight attendant took one look at Angus and gushed, "What a beautiful dog!" There was no way she was going to let this "poor creature" fly all squished up in the Economy Class, so she moved us to First Class.

All my stress disappeared.

It was quite a sight: Angus sprawled out at my feet with more room than he knew what to do with; the flight attendant, sitting on a nearby chair, facing Angus, unable to take her eyes off him; and me, eating stuffed chicken breast off a china plate, sitting in a large leather chair.

It was a night flight, so after dinner I tried to sleep. We needed to get used to the German time difference as quickly as possible and be rested enough to row the next day. As I drifted in and out of consciousness, I woke up to the flight attendant cooing at Angus and saying things like "he's such a gentle soul," or "our friend, Angus."

This was my first encounter with the "extreme dog lover." There are people in this world who are absolutely crazy about dogs. They can't control themselves. They are compelled to touch your dog, talk to your dog, interpret what he's doing, and, most important, tell you everything about their own dogs. I have met many, many of these dog people, but she was the first.

The flight went smoothly, but when we arrived in Munich, we discovered that all of our luggage had been lost between connecting flights. It was a rough few hours as we waited in lineups to fill out forms about our luggage.

Our hotel managers were waiting for us at the airport so they could drive us to the inn.

The inn we were staying at was a family-run business that had been going for three generations. Everything was small and dark and set at weird angles. I shared a room with Meghan. The room was tiny and had two twin beds — smaller than twin, almost like child-size beds. By now I was completely comfortable sharing a room with Meghan, and we laughed together at how ridiculous the room was.

The beds were actually pushed together, so the first thing we did was pull them apart so we each had some space. When either of us wanted to be inside our own head, we would put on earphones and listen to music, but mostly we watched German MTV and laughed at the odd shows that aired there.

I was not comfortable in the hotel itself. The layout was so strange; doors were not where you'd expect, and there were stairs in odd locations and at odd angles. I was often confused, bumping into things or tripping over something. Luckily I had Angus, so he minimized the number of mishaps, but it was still unfamiliar and frustrating. I hated that feeling, not realizing that it would pass. It reminded me of being in our new house and the stress I dealt with there. I was in a new chapter of my life, and I did not want to return to those feelings. I thought I would never learn the layout of the hotel. And every time I made a mistake, I felt embarrassed and frustrated with myself. As in Montreal, I wondered why I was putting myself through hardship and I couldn't wait to go home.

I have learned over the years that you do get used to it. It takes a few days to adjust to unknown environments, but things quickly become so familiar that before you know it, the once unfamiliar becomes a place that you will miss.

The Adaptive Team was the first of the Canadian teams to arrive. The Women's Team was coming a couple of days after us, and the men a day after that. Once everyone arrived, we would occupy every room in the hotel. Dinners were awesome for the first couple of nights: meats with rich sauces, mashed potatoes, pizza, and we even got decadent desserts. Laura assured us this would all change once the women arrived.

I had no idea what to expect. I didn't know anything about elite sport and didn't know any of the National Team rowers. This event was a qualifier for the Olympics, so Rowing Canada sent more boats than they might have in other years. Almost every boat configuration was represented in both the men's and women's programs: eights, fours, pairs, quads, doubles, and singles. There was also a lightweight program on both the men's and women's sides. They raced fours, doubles, pairs, and singles. My teammates knew their names and their accomplishments, but they did not really know them personally. Laura had gone to school with the woman racing the lightweight single, so they were sharing a room, and Meghan had raced the Manitoba eight with a woman who was rowing in the quad. Other than that, the rest of the teams were strangers to us.

Laura was right about things changing. Once the Women's Team nutritionist spoke to the kitchen, there were no more sauces, no more rich foods, and definitely no more desserts. Everything was broiled or steamed and super healthy.

Some of the lightweight women carried food scales around with them to weigh exactly how much food they were allowed to consume. Some of them ate things like lettuce with tomato sauce for dinner to make sure they kept their weight low. I couldn't imagine that kind of pressure on top of the ever-growing fear I had of competing on the world stage.

The men's eating habits were just as fascinating as the women's. The kitchen staff could not cook enough food to keep them happy and resorted to making pizza after pizza following the main course to help satisfy the men's appetites. No wonder, they would row up to 40 kilometres a day.

The able-bodied team (AB) operated separately from us. They didn't sit with us or talk to us, and I'm pretty sure they didn't even look at us. I definitely did not feel like I fit in with them. They were all super fit and confident, and I was neither. As much as I had improved my fitness level, I was nowhere near as fit as they, and I was embarrassed to be in the same room. We did our own thing, and they did theirs.

The race course was about a 30-minute drive from the hotel. It was the *Regattastrecke,* or regatta course, from the 1972 Munich Olympics, exactly the same setup as the Montreal Basin. The grandstand was enormous, and there were boat bays as far as the eye could see with rack upon rack of boats.

We were all given photo ID, accreditation that allowed us access to the venue. Each entrance was heavily staffed so no spectators would be able to get in. The photographer asked me if he could make an accreditation ID tag for Angus, and we clipped it to his dog collar. He wore it every day along with his maple leaf bandana. Pretty soon everyone knew Angus by name.

Angus had a tent that he could hang out in while I was rowing. I would leave him with a bowl of water and his chew toy. He was a celebrity wherever we went. People were always taking photos of him, and by the end of the week complete strangers were saying hi to him by name.

One afternoon, one of the French coaches was trying to communicate something to us, but we couldn't understand what he was saying. Meghan told me that he was pointing at Angus and motioning in the direction of the Jumbotron by the grandstand. We finally figured out that he wanted us to follow him. He had noticed the day before that we had left Angus's chew toy on the grass and he had hidden it by the grandstand so that he could return it to us!

Another day we were at the hotel and the front desk received a phone call from the rowing venue. "Don't worry," the caller told the hotel manager, "we found Angus, and he's here with us."

The manager could see me sitting across the foyer with Angus beside me. "No, you didn't. He's right here," the manager replied. It seemed some poor German shepherd had been abducted, mistaken for Angus!

As the race day approached, we started to taper our training in preparation. A taper is when you gradually decrease the intensity of training to allow your body time to recover and build up strength for the competition. We did shorter, more intense practices, which left us a lot of downtime. We spent it watching DVDs on laptops, playing cards, playing fetch with Angus in the back, or going for a soak in the whirlpool. There were bikes for rent at the hotel, but no one (not even the ABs) was allowed to take them out for fear of someone getting injured. We were also not allowed to go into Munich to walk around in case we got too tired or too distracted.

The first few days at the course were quiet. Not all the countries' teams had arrived yet, including the Americans. They had become our adversaries because of a blog post one of their team members had written. In it, he put down the Canadian adaptive four from the previous year, basically saying Canada hadn't deserved to win the bronze. As a training technique to help us train harder, we had developed a very strong desire to beat the USA, particularly that one athlete. It was a good call for Laura to pull out in the boat when we needed a little extra steam.

Out at practice we rowed up near the German adaptive team. I had the blackout goggles on (mandatory even for practice on the course) so I couldn't see them, but I could hear them. Their sound threw me off my rhythm — they sounded fierce. I didn't know what their coxswain was saying to them, but it sounded like he was screaming "Diiiiiiiiiiiiiiie! Diiiiiiiiiiiiiiie!" like a death-metal singer. It was very intimidating, along with the sound of their oars being pulled through the water — WHOOSH... WHOOSH... And based on what the rest of my team was saying, they were really good.

When the USA finally arrived, Meghan said hi when they first passed her and they walked right past her. That just added fuel to our fire. Then the British arrived, and I felt the tension mount. They had won our event every year since it began.

Finally, it was time for the first heat. There were 15 countries, which meant there would be a heat, a repechage (a second chance to make the semi-final), a semi-final, and a final. The top two finishers out of the six in each heat would go straight to the semi-final; the rest would go to repechage. We had to make the top two.

We had a meeting to go over our race plan one more time. Then Laura sat with each of us individually to hear what we needed in the race plan. It was a crucial part of our strategy for her to know what would motivate us when we needed to push. I told her I was doing this to make my kids proud of me.

There were two heats. The first heat had Great Britain and Germany. We were in the second heat, and so was the USA. We were happy to be doing the first one without the two biggest threats next to us. And we were ready to take on the US.

It ended up being a good race for us. We got out in front right from the start and held the lead the whole way down the course. The USA finished second, quite far behind us. We wonder if they took it easy to save energy for the semi-final, since the semi-final would determine who qualified for Beijing.

Tony, Laura, and me in Munich

Germany had beaten Great Britain, which shocked us. They really were a threat. But then an announcement was made that after officials had weighed Germany's boat, it was actually lighter than was allowed. I assumed that meant they were disqualified. "Thank goodness!" I thought. I was so excited that we wouldn't have to race them.

When I asked Meghan if that were the case, she said, "I hope not. I'm dying to race them!"

I was taken aback by her response. I wished I could think that way, but it takes time to develop that that kind of attitude.

As it turned out, Germany just had to add weight to their boat and race the repecharge to earn their place in the semi-final. They qualified easily.

We had to race the USA again in our semi-final lineup. This race, the top three would move on to the final and qualify to compete at the Paralympics. Finishing in the top three would also mean that we qualified for carding from Sports Canada. Under a program called the Athlete Assistance Program (AAP), Sports Canada provides government funding for qualified or "carded" athletes to support them in their training. It was a big race.

Eamonn had arrived the day before (the kids were staying with their godparents). He was more nervous that I was! He wasn't sure if he'd ever have the opportunity to see me represent Canada again, so he made sure he was there to watch. The semi-final was the big race for him, more so than the final, because this was the one that could rank us in the top six in the world.

We won our semi-final.

As we gathered by the boat to debrief, I felt amazing. Laura had recorded her calls throughout the race, so we crowded around and listened, reliving the moments that were forgotten in the mayhem of racing. The race was hell, but listening to it afterward gave me goosebumps. It was so worth it. We were among the top six in the world. We would receive funding to train, and we qualified for Beijing. I thought all of that would be enough for me, but we still had the final to race, and now I wanted a medal.

The nerves returned, and I was not looking forward to the final. I enjoyed the training in between — no pressure to perform, I didn't have to push myself as far, and I didn't have to worry about failing. Meghan, on the other hand, looked forward to it all week. She was always saying things like, "Bring it on!" or "I wish we could just race right now!"

I continued to admire her attitude.

I did not sleep well the night before the final race. I wrote out the technical pieces I was working on and visualized the race plan, but I was feeling nauseated like never before.

In the morning, the hotel was buzzing; everyone was getting ready for semis or finals depending on their category. People gathered around the two public computers in the lobby waiting to email home. Only a few people had laptops, and the wireless Internet signal was weak. My team sat on the sofa around a laptop watching a Hugh Grant movie.

Our race wasn't until 4:00 p.m., so I put it out of my mind until it was time to drive to the course. I didn't allow myself to think about it because I knew the thought would make me sick. In the other races, I had felt pretty confident that we would make the top two, and the process had felt like a learning experience as we went. But the next race was to determine the best in the world, and I really wanted to win a medal. It was scary to be taking on a risk like that. What if we lost?

Eventually, the time came to go. When we got to the course, I had a hard time eating my packed lunch. My stomach was queasy, and my mouth was dry. I knew I would need the energy, but it was hard to swallow.

I managed to eat half of my sandwich and an apple — not exactly a pre-race meal. As in previous competitions, we kept to a strict schedule for pre-race rituals.

At 2:30 p.m., we double-checked all our gear because people had been known to tamper with equipment. The oars were at the right length, the bolts on the boat were tight, the slides for the seats were clean, and the shoes were tightly fixed in place.

Pop music blared from nearby speakers. I watched in awe as some athletes ran by wearing garbage bags, trying to lose a few last ounces to make weight. Laura had already weighed in; if she were lighter than 110 pounds, she would have had to carry sandbags with her to make up the difference in weight.

At 3:00 p.m., we took our final bathroom break.

At 3:15 p.m., we took the oars down to the dock.

At 3:25 p.m., we walked the boat down to the dock, and an official checked each of our identification tags to make sure we didn't have a ringer! It surprised me to learn what some athletes do to win.

A FISA official approved my goggles, and we pushed off. As we started our warm-up, my nausea grew and my hands started shaking. I really didn't want to do this. I wondered what I had been thinking; this wasn't worth it at all. Other people were sitting at home, relaxed, enjoying the day. I was so scared. I was so nervous. I was sure I was going to throw up. This was going to hurt so much. I didn't want to mess up. All this and more went screaming through my mind.

As the warm-up progressed and the strokes got harder and faster, I felt the nerves start to subside. The warm-up forced my body to prepare. I remembered that I could control this feeling and transform it into power. But I wasn't fully buying into it yet…

I felt so tired already. I panicked and eased off in the warm-up, not giving my full effort on the hard strokes. I figured I would go hard again after a bit of a rest. But before I knew it, we were being called up to the start.

We backed the boat in to the gate, little strokes a few at a time, a little to the left, one more to the right. We listened intently and followed Laura's directions. We were in and we were ready to go. Laura's voice came in loud and clear over the speakers: "Sit ready."

We all slid forward, our arms straight, legs bent, shins perpendicular to the boat and ready to pull.

"Russia! Canada! Great Britain! Germany! United States of America! Italy!" The officials called to each country over the loudspeaker. "Attention…"

This was it. Any time now. A few more seconds passed.

"Row!"

And before I knew it, we were going full speed. I focused on

Laura's voice, ready to do whatever she told me. In the background I kept telling myself two things: I have to hold my knees down, and I have to swing out. Hold my knees. Swing out. Hold. Swing. I repeated it over and over to myself all the way down the course.

Laura's voice cut in to my mantra. "That's it Canada, long and strong!" She sounded confident, as though things were going well. Germany was out in front, and everyone else was vying for second place.

"Accelerate that outside arm... It's working!" she called. "You're moving into second... with a bunch of other boats!"

It's so close that I can hear everyone beside us, and I can hear the excitement in Laura's voice. It gave me a new energy. I held my knees down, I swung out, and I pulled as hard as I could.

"Canada we need to pull harder, Vicky, Do it for Tarabh and Ceili! Meghan, goin' for Canada! Scott, goin' for Canada! Tony, you're an athlete! Stand on those legs!"

I jumped on my foot-stretchers and pulled on that oar with everything I had. I imagined Tarabh and Ceili telling people that their mom won a medal for Canada. I only started this as a hobby, I thought, and look how far I'd come! I got another charge of energy.

The pain was slowing me down, but the voice in my head got louder: "Hold the knees; swing out." I couldn't sit up straight, it just hurt too much. I couldn't hold on much longer. Where was that finish line?

I could hear the crowd in the grandstands. Everyone was going crazy! I knew Eamonn must be on the edge of his seat. My sister, Lesley, was also there, and I could imagine her screaming.

It was down to the last ten strokes. Great Britain was in second place, and everyone else was battling for third.

"We're going up again." Laura screamed, "Go! Everything! Now!"

"Just don't catch a crab" was all I could think. I was holding on for dear life.

We crossed the finish line, and Laura called us down. I thought we might have been the third beep across the line, but I wasn't sure.

I was gasping for breath, doubled over. "How'd we do?"

I could tell Laura was smiling when she said, "Third."

Sitting at the finish line with those ridiculous goggles on, I was in shock. I could hear the crowd and the German brass band playing the victory music as the winners were announced: "Germany... Great Britain... Canada!" Scott cheered and splashed water forward over all of us.

We rowed over to the dock where the medal ceremony took place in front of the grandstand. As soon as my hand touched the dock I ripped off my goggles. A.R. was there waiting for us, beaming. She was laughing, and she was hoarse from screaming.

"Thanks, you guys, that was so much fun!" she said and gave us each a big hug. I couldn't believe I had achieved everything I'd set out to do, and more.

The lucky loonie we dropped at the finish line

As we stood there with our medals, the German national anthem played, and I couldn't help but imagine what it would be like to hear Canada's national anthem playing for us. But I let that thought go quickly; I was so thrilled to have won bronze.

Rowing Canada gave us a big Canadian flag to hold up for photos. Meghan told me that Eamonn and Lesley had rushed up to the fence, and she brought me over to them. I gave them each a big hug over the top of the fence. We couldn't stop laughing.

There was a great celebration in Munich that night. Eamonn told everyone who would listen — people we met in bars, the hotel staff. When we flew back to Toronto, he and I flew separately — I was travelling with my team. When I got to Customs at the airport in Toronto, the agent asked me why I had been away. I told her, and the tone of her voice brightened.

"Oh, your husband came through here earlier! He's very proud!"

I laughed. What a great time in my life.

CHAPTER 13

I start to think that I have jumped the gun with my effort in this race. I don't think I can hold up this power to the end, but I can't ease off — my race plan was to increase my effort with each 250 metres. Even if I were to maintain my current effort, I would consider this a failure, I have to pick it up. I definitely can't ease off. I know that if we can cross the 500-metre mark in second position, we can hold it to the finish. I had to work toward smaller goals to manage this race.

"All we have to do is cross the 500 in second place," I keep telling myself. "We're almost there."

I returned from Munich, put my medal in a drawer, and started a new teaching job. I managed to get myself out of that awful situation by applying to new schools. In my applications, I outlined how I teach despite vision loss. Trying to move to a new school was so competitive that I figured that even though there probably wouldn't be anyone interested in hiring a person with a disability, at least I would be educating people.

To my surprise, there was one principal who saw the value in having me teach at her school. Andrea Rowan hired me to be a role model for the students of Gledhill Public School and to teach them about empathy.

It was great to be teaching again. I had 12 students in grades five and six who had a variety of learning challenges. They were respectful of my disability, and I was a great role model for them. I was proof: how you perform at school does not have to dictate your future. Who would have thought the kid who failed gym class would one day win a medal for Canada?

In December I was invited to the Rowing Canada Awards banquet and was named "Female Adaptive Athlete of the Year." Eamonn and I attended the dinner, and I received a plaque with my name engraved on it. Meanwhile, I knew I had to do more if I wanted to win gold in Beijing.

Winning the Female Adaptive Athlete of the Year

I was receiving funding from Sport Canada because of our success in Munich, so I was able to work with a personal trainer (gyms and fitness classes were not accessible for me), and I was also able to take taxis to rowing practices after school. When I wasn't at a camp with my team, I would train at Argos. The trick was finding someone to row with. They had a senior women's competitive team, but I couldn't try out for it because it conflicted with the NART schedule. Their big race would be the Henley, and I couldn't train and compete with them around those dates in August because I'd be training and competing with my own team. It was tough to find someone who was willing to complete the workouts outlined by the national coach, but who was doing it just for fun.

Fortunately I found someone, Alyssa Vito, the rower from Michigan University whom I'd met when I first started adaptive rowing. She was always offering her time to help adaptive rowers at the club. She volunteered countless hours to row with me and coach me one-on-one whenever she was home. I also bought myself a newer erg so that I could train more effectively at home in the mornings.

I competed and won in the indoor erg competition again for 2008 and knocked 5 seconds off my time from the year before — a huge accomplishment. In the middle of my race, when I heard the commentator announce that I would be competing in Beijing later that year, it only made me pull harder.

As a team we decided to fund our own training camp. We weren't scheduled to train together through Rowing Canada until March, and we wanted to keep on top of things. We booked a trip to Miami, where Laura had connections to a club including a boat and a coach. We trained for ten days in Miami, and we knew we were getting an edge on the competition.

Tarabh took karate lessons at Dragonz Martial Arts, very close to our house. The owner, Marvin Prashad, was a phenomenal athlete, and the way he motivated and pushed his students to excellence was something I needed. He did personal training on the side, so I hired him to help get me in better shape.

It became clear very quickly that I had a lot of work to do. He told me that my cardio fitness was weak and that I needed to build up muscle. By the end of each 60-minute session, I had worked so hard that I could barely walk the next day. It sounds crazy, but I accomplished things I would never have dreamed I could do with his motivation to push limits.

The four training in Miami

One of the rewards of becoming a competitive athlete was meeting "outliers," people who are driven and who will overcome any challenge in order to succeed and achieve their goals. Marvin was one of these people. He knew not only what muscle groups to target and how to increase fitness levels but also how to get inside my mind and spark my desire to achieve.

One day, I had already been working for 40 minutes, hard training. My arms felt like dead weight at my sides. I had nothing left. At that point Marvin wanted me to do seated rows, which meant making the rowing motion with my arms while holding weights. I could barely lift the weights, never mind do the sets. I have always been really hard on myself and I don't like to quit, but I knew there was no way I could do these sets. I told Marvin, but he would not allow me to quit.

"You *can* do it," he insisted. "This is when it counts. This is when you see what you're made of. Come on, let's go."

I could tell there was no room for debate. I was going to do those sets.

With Marvin's encouragement throughout, I finished the set. When I weakened, he would shout, "Pick it up!" and my instinct to quit would be overridden. I hurt, but the thrill of completing the exercise gave me such a high. I had no idea I could push myself to that level. I would have bet money that I wouldn't be able to finish that workout! As the weeks went on he taught me over and over again about mental discipline and pushing through my perceived limits.

He pushed me more and more each week. We even started doing some martial arts to help develop my arms and shoulders. I could feel how much stronger I was getting. I was starting to feel more like an athlete. I knew I still had a long way to go before I would feel satisfied, and I still didn't feel comfortable in a unisuit, but I was getting there!

In March, I was working with a punching bag when I felt something odd in my shoulder. It didn't really hurt; it just felt like something was not right. After the workout my right forearm was swollen and was bright red. I figured I had strained the muscle. I iced it and continued with my training, but every time I did a workout the same thing happened.

My doctor was puzzled and directed me to my rowing coach. My coach was also unsure. She told me if it didn't hurt that I could keep rowing. I didn't know what was wrong but I knew something wasn't right — I could feel it. I started to get aggressive massage therapy to try and relax the muscle but that didn't work either. Finally I went to a doctor of sports medicine who suggested I get some tests done.

One of the tests was an ultrasound so we could rule out a blood clot, even though a clot was highly unlikely. The technician didn't speak English very well, and after she looked at the screen she bolted out of the room looking for the doctor.

I was told to get to an emergency room immediately and that I had a blood clot in my shoulder, as a result of aggressive weight training. The doctors put me on blood thinners and, until they could determine the correct dosage, they were injected through a needle in my stomach every single day. A nurse would come to my home to administer the needle. It was supposed to take seven to ten days to figure out the correct dosage, and in the meantime I was to take a break from training. I figured seven days off wouldn't make a huge difference. I was doing more than double the training I had done the year before.

Then a bomb dropped. There was a woman out in British Columbia who had been rowing as an able-bodied athlete, but who qualified for our boat. Her disability was a club foot. Apparently she was fast, and she was coming after my seat. If she beat me in seat racing, I wouldn't be going to Beijing.

Eighteen needles later — and 18 days of not training — the doctors figured out the correct dosage of blood thinner and I started taking pills rather than needles.

I resumed training, but I would never get back those 18 days. I imagined my competition in BC, training for those two and a half weeks, getting an edge on me. I had to make sure I was on my game at every practice and every training session from that day on. In just one month I would have to race her for a spot to compete in Beijing.

In the meantime, the excitement about the Games was building. I did interviews for CBC Radio and Global TV. Surprisingly, although I was extremely nervous, I came across as confident and well-spoken. I was amazed that yet another skill that I had thought was a weakness of mine turned out to be strength.

I also had the opportunity to sit in on a committee to evaluate Canada's Paralympic clothing line and get a sneak preview of what it would look like. Learning about the clothing was so exciting. Just as Olympians have an Opening Ceremony outfit, a medal outfit, and so on, Paralympians also receive a suitcase full of Canada gear. It gave me a chill to think of wearing those clothes and walking into the different ceremonies.

After having our accreditation photo taken
(We did our own!)

We also had a meeting where we saw photos of the athletes' village, the same village the Olympic athletes stay in. It sounded phenomenal! How cool would it be just to visit the village, never mind to be a guest there? I couldn't allow things to really sink in. It was all so overwhelming and unbelievable that I had to shut off my emotions about the whole thing — especially since I wasn't officially going yet.

June arrived, and it was time to seat race. There would be five races in total. Tony was also fighting for his seat against another man. Because of certain Paralympic rules around what combination of disabilities was allowed in the boat, Tony and I would be racing as a pair against the two new athletes.

Here's how it worked: There were two boats of four. In the first boat, Meghan and Scott would be the constants. In the second boat, two able-bodied athletes would be the constants. The competing pairs would switch in and out of each boat. If our boat won by 2 seconds, we would get a score of +2. If their boat won, they would get that score. Over the five races we would add up all the scores to determine who moved a boat fastest.

This type of racing was so foreign to me. I didn't like it at all because it wasn't a team effort. Tony and I were on our own, and we were fighting for survival, not competition. It was not a very positive energy at all. There was tension between us and Meghan and Scott as they wondered who would end up being faster — I know they wanted whoever might get them gold in Beijing. It was to be expected; this was high-performance sport.

Initially I was feeling unsure. I'm sorry to say I was starting to shy away from the fight, and I did not give everything I had. That was the easy way out. I wouldn't have to hurt if I didn't risk everything. In the first race I was in our four with Scott and Meghan. We beat the other boat by 2 seconds, but for the next race, our competitors were with Scott and Meghan, and they beat us by 2.5 seconds. That was all I needed. My competitiveness kicked in. I decided to end it then and there. I was going to make our coach's decision easy. I was in the able-bodied boat again, the one that kept losing. The goal could have been to lose by less, but I decided to take it further and make this boat win this time. Tony was thinking the same thing. As we sat at the start line and my nerves kicked in, Tony called up, "Alright, Vic, let's keep the four together!"

There was no way I was ending my journey here, and I was going to show our coach that this decision wasn't even close. We were the obvious choice.

We fought with such strength that it shouldn't have surprised me when we won, but it did! We not only beat them, but we beat them by 5 seconds! The racing continued, but that race put us well over the top. They couldn't make up those 5 seconds. I was overwhelmed with pride as I realized the discipline and strength it took to pull that off. My confidence was building exponentially, and my thirst for competition was growing too. That was one race. Imagine if I put that kind of focus into my training...

There was so much relief when the team was named, and it remained the five of us who had won in Munich — Laura, Meghan, Scott, Tony, and me. We were the first Canadian Paralympic Rowing Team. We were making history! And we were so strong that we knew we had a shot at gold.

Later that summer, the Royal Canadian Henley was featuring our race as a big event. The US Paralympic Team was going to race us, and the winner would be given a trophy as well as medals. I thought it would be amazing if Tarabh and Ceili could one day show their children the trophy that would sit in the clubhouse in St. Catharines.

Eamonn had organized a bus load of fans to come down to St. Catharines to watch the race. All of our friends and family were there. My best friend from university, Bev Lategan, had moved to Vancouver, but she happened to be in Toronto for this event, and she took the bus down even though she knew she wouldn't get to talk to me. Friends I hadn't seen for years all piled on a yellow school bus to come out and cheer for us.

We had raced the Americans earlier in the summer and had won one race and lost one. We knew that with all our extra training since then, we were even faster this time.

We were in the gates, the blackout goggles were on. The official began the usual announcement: "USA... Canada... Attention..." Then there was a high-pitched beep. We all waited for the "go," but it didn't come.

The next couple of seconds felt like an eternity. I wondered if we were supposed to just go without the verbal command — I couldn't see the lights. No one said anything. We didn't want to get a yellow card for a false start. Then we heard the American boat start and Laura yelled, "Go!" so we went.

The lights had come on to tell us to go, but the officials forgot that they need to call out the start for their visually impaired athletes at adaptive events. It was okay; we were neck and neck with the USA, and we would overtake them soon. Our race plan unfolded, and we executed everything just as we had planned, but as we pulled ahead of the USA, they pulled back on us. If we took a seat, then they took a seat back. "Taking a seat" is a rough measurement we use in rowing; it means seeing one rower in line with another in the next boat, then advancing to line up with the person in the next seat. It was a brutal race; we were beside each other the whole way down the course. We decided to sprint early. So did they. We just couldn't get in front of them.

We heard the grandstand, and I could tell that it was packed. The crowd was split, chanting "Ca-na-da!" or "U-S-A!" The sound got louder, and it was so exciting! I knew I had to keep going as hard as I could right to the end.

We surged over the line, and it was a photo finish. Both boats stopped, and we all sat waiting for the results. I heard one of the rowers in the USA boat exclaim, "What a race!" The announcement finally came over the speakers: "Canada, 3:35.36; United States of America, 3:35.35." They had won by 1/100 of a second.

Devastating. But we sat tall and rowed proudly away while the USA team climbed onto the podium to get their medals. And the trophy.

I didn't actually get to see Eamonn and the kids or anyone who came to see us race. The team was heading right back to training camp, and the spectators were all getting back on the bus home. Tarabh and Ceili were not too disappointed. They didn't understand the importance of the race and were probably glad to be doing something other than sitting in the stands.

After we debriefed with A.R., we had a better perspective. Some unfortunate things cost us the race, like the awkward start. Our final sprint also needed to be more defined. Had those elements been stronger, it would have been us on the podium. We learned from our experience, and we would be that much better in Beijing.

Over the next month, A.R. gave us some tricks that we could use if the same situation presented itself in Beijing. We worked on a stronger finish so that if it came down to it, we could pull ahead in the last 250 metres. We were confident as we got on the plane for Beijing.

We were interviewed for a newspaper before we left, and the press quoted Laura's sage words: "Nothing makes you hungrier for gold than losing by 0.01 seconds." She was right. We were coming after the US and the rest of the world.

CHAPTER 14

No matter how physically fit you are, you have to be mentally prepared to fight all the obstacles that are thrown at you in a race. Your body thinks it's dying, the other boats are either ahead of you or bearing down on you, and there's no room for error. It's only 1,000 metres, and it's an all-out sprint. If your mind is not "on" that day, all your physical training is useless.

While I was physically preparing for Beijing, I was continuing to have my mental toughness tested.

In January, my trial date for the cab driver incident came up. I really did not want to stand in front of a courtroom and tell the story, but I felt sure I was right, and I knew that I needed to speak up in order to help other people. Not all visually impaired people would be strong enough to speak up and defend the right to use a service dog. I was lucky that I was able to, so even though it was hard, I felt I had a responsibility to do so. At the trial, the driver showed no remorse and offered no explanation for his behaviour. He was fined $2,000 and summoned to appear before a licensing tribunal.

Just a week later I was downtown by myself with Angus after a dentist appointment, and I tried to hail a cab. I stood at a major intersection with my hand up as cars rushed by. I realized I couldn't tell if there was a cab in the distance, but I just kept my hand up.

I felt silly standing with my arm up in the middle of Queen Street, but finally a car pulled up in front of me. As I reached out to find the door handle, the car accelerated and jerked forward, braking suddenly. Confused, I looked around and realized the light was red at the intersection. As I opened the door, the driver said, "No dogs."

I got in anyway, telling him that Angus was a guide dog. The driver apologized, but it was clear to me that if the light had been green, he would have been long gone. I wondered how many other taxis out there would do the same thing and wondered how long I might have been stranded there.

It happened when I ordered a taxi as well. Drivers pulled up to my house, and they either tried to drive away when they saw I had a dog, or they were very hostile with me. I started telling the dispatch operator that I had a dog to eliminate the surprise, but it still happened.

These kinds of incidents caused me so much anxiety that I put off doing things just so I wouldn't have to go through the stress of dealing with these people. I was right back where I used to be, afraid to go out and making excuses.

The situation got worse because it started happening in other places. When our team decided to fund our own training camp in Miami, we had a hard time finding a hotel that would allow guide dogs! One manager told me that we could stay, but I would have to pay $500 to have the room cleaned after we left (this is also against the law). We finally found a place that understood that guide dogs were an exception to the "no pets" rule, but in the process of searching, I filed two complaints with the Department of Justice. Through mediation, I asked that the two hotels I'd dealt with fully train their staff in dealing with people who have disabilities. They also had to put up "Service Animals Welcome" signs, and they each made a donation to the Fidelco Guide Dog School.

These small victories felt good, but they didn't undo the damage to my confidence.

The issues continued in businesses around the city of Toronto:

"You can't come in here."

"Dogs are not allowed."

"No pets in here."

"You have to sit outside."

"No! No! No!"

Sometimes nothing was said, but I felt the tension. Those times were the worst because I couldn't start a dialogue to explain. Sometimes a host sat me in a remote corner of the restaurant and claimed that everything else was booked. Sometimes I got up and left because the situation was so uncomfortable.

Imagine the stress generated when I had to go to an unfamiliar business for a meeting. It was bad enough when I was with family and friends, but worse when I was meeting strangers and worrying about making impressions. The anticipation of entering a place prompted high anxiety, and I often felt nauseous just thinking about it. Sometimes I was in the mood to take it on; other days it made me want to stay in.

Another frustrating and annoying part of walking with a guide dog was the fear that some people have of dogs —

especially German shepherds. As much as I would try to ignore it, when people are running away screaming or leaping out of your way in horror day after day, it starts to wear on you.

The upside was that all that frustration with people and anger about why things had to be so complicated were channelled into power when I got on the erg. My training sessions had come a long way in the last year, and I was getting stronger and able to handle more speed.

CHAPTER 15

"That's 500 down," Laura informs us. We've reached the halfway point.

"Game number two," I think to myself. One of the psychological tricks is to have a reset point in the race where you put what's happened behind you and enter a whole new phase. It's an opportunity to take a new approach, and you can imagine a new wave of energy. My excitement grew. I knew that once I passed the 500-metre mark I could make it to the end. With another 250 metres down, it was time to pick up the intensity again, and I did.

Angus was awesome on the 11-hour flight to Beijing. The flight attendants were in love with him. They even set up an area for him to relieve himself, covered with garbage bags. But when I brought him over and gave him the command to go ("Angus, get busy!"), all he did was lie down. He was so well-trained that he would not go indoors. The poor guy held it for the entire flight.

When we got off the plane, we attracted quite a crowd. People stared and gasped and grabbed cameras to take photos of him. The crowd grew, and they walked alongside us as we travelled through the airport. Meghan told me that one man ran ahead of us and started filming us as he scurried backwards. I kept waiting for him to fall, but he must have done this before. The crowd could not get enough. They stayed with us the entire time, a giant entourage surrounding us as we walked. And they were all there when poor Angus couldn't take any more waiting and urinated all over the airport floor. Surprisingly, there were no audible reactions to this. Everyone just continued to stare, mesmerized.

A typical entourage that followed me in Beijing

Meghan and I frantically mopped up after Angus. She was always so helpful both with my dogs and with me. She had become like a sister to me, and my team a second family. I kept expecting someone to come up and speak to us about the incident (or arrest us!), but no one did. I had no idea what their understanding of guide dogs was. Allison had arranged all the details for Angus's travel and entry into the country. Apparently

China had just passed the law recently, in 2008, that guide dogs were permitted in public places. This law came into effect because of the Paralympic Games, which had brought much more awareness to accessibility issues than ever before. China also opened its first guide-dog school in 2008, and they had placed six dogs with clients. Angus was the seventh guide dog in China, and so far he was a smashing success!

I had already decided that I would not be using Angus outside of the athletes' village. The law was too new for people to really understand it; Canada had passed it 30 years ago, and apparently people still didn't always understand it.

After getting our luggage, our team was informed that we had to go to a separate room with Angus. We were all confused because the bus was waiting to take us into the village. We waited in a room with about 20 officials from the airport. They didn't seem to be doing much of anything other than staring and taking photos. No one approached us or spoke to us, so after 15 minutes we found someone who spoke English, and they told us they didn't need anything else. We're still not sure what that detour was about; I'm convinced it was just a photo opportunity. We went out and climbed on board the bus, and the entourage reached their cameras up inside the bus to grab the last couple of photos before we pulled away.

At the village we were given our photo identification, which had to be swiped each time we entered the village. Also, each time you entered, your bags went through a security scan just like at the airport. There were Chinese police armed with rifles, guarding every entrance to the village.

The village itself was spectacular inside. It covered 66 square hectares, and even with my tiny spotlight of vision I could see it was even more beautiful than I had imagined. The walkways were interlocking bricks bordered by beautifully landscaped gardens containing waterfalls, statues, and sculpted hedges. Throughout the village was the Paralympic symbol, carved on sculptures and in plants.

There were 42 apartment buildings in total. Canada had such a large team that we had a whole apartment building for ourselves. Laura, Meghan, and I shared one of the apartments. It was small but very modern and nicely decorated. Artwork depicting the various Olympic and Paralympic sports had been supplied by local school children. We had a couch and table in the living area. Meghan and I shared a room, and Laura had her own.

The one really odd thing was the bathroom. The shower was not separated from the rest of the bathroom as we're used to in North America. Instead, the showerhead came out of the wall, and the water ran directly onto the floor! There was no lip, no change in flooring, not even a slope in the floor. When you showered, the entire bathroom floor was flooded. It seemed, however, that the Chinese recognized the issue because each bathroom came equipped with a squeegee. After your shower, you could squeegee the floor water over to the drain. Of course you never got all the water out, so walking into the bathroom was always treacherous.

Waiting for each of us in our apartment were beige suitcases emblazoned with the giant word "CANADA" in red letters on the side and a giant red maple leaf on the front. Each one had a tag with someone's name on it, and Laura and Meghan sorted them out for us. The cases were full of Team Canada gear, and it felt like Christmas when we opened them up and went through everything. We tried everything on immediately, planned what we would wear on different days, and decided which pieces were our favourites. Everything was red and white and gold. We each received two T-shirts, two tank tops, two long-sleeved shirts and a short-sleeved shirt, two pairs of shorts, and two pairs of pants. While we were in the village, we were allowed to wear team-issued clothing only, and we were not permitted to wear anything that had a logo. Thankfully we all liked the clothing, and, more important, it was comfortable and would keep us cool in the Beijing heat.

Next we headed to the food building for lunch. That was an experience! It seated over 5,000 people and offered every food imaginable. I had brought peanut butter with me, thinking they wouldn't have it in China, but at the food building they had everything from peanut butter to cream cheese, tzatziki, and hummus — whatever you wanted.

In the centre was a bin filled with hundreds of bananas and oranges, and it was refilled often throughout the day. I heard that just fewer than 1,000,000 bananas were consumed during the Paralympic Games. There was a food station representing every part of the world, and everything was open 24 hours a day. So if you wanted noodles for breakfast, you could go to the Asian counter. If you wanted pizza or pasta for dinner, the Italian counter was open, and so on. They had every type of fruit under the sun and even had artists come in and create ornate sculptures out of some of the fruit.

Despite all that, our team stuck to a very strict diet and counted down the days until we were done racing and could sample all this great food. Breakfast was always eggs and toast with fruit; lunch was usually a plain chicken breast with salad; and dinner was usually pasta. I often had to force it down because I knew I needed the fuel. I was not looking forward to consuming more food when we were done; I was looking forward to not having to eat as much! It had become annoying, having to eat eggs every morning to make sure I was fuelled for practice. I would have loved to just have a coffee and a croissant.

Our coach kept us on a work-like schedule and advised us to treat our time here like a job. This was the plan to avoid distractions — and there were plenty of those!

We met every morning for breakfast and then had a team meeting where we discussed strategies or visualized our race plan. We were free for an hour then we travelled to the course, almost an hour away. We practiced, ate lunch at a cafeteria, and then travelled back to the village. This was the routine every day.

I did take the time to appreciate what I was doing while we practiced. Scott and I had both decided that we would be retiring from rowing after the Paralympics. It was a lot to manage along with a career and family. Besides, once I won a medal at the Paralympics, I would really feel like I had accomplished more than what I had set out to do.

It felt so lonely to be on the opposite side of the planet from Eamonn and the kids, especially with such a big time difference. I don't think I would have made it if not for the fact that about a month before we left, I had nominated Eamonn to be a torchbearer. I described all the support he had given me, and he was chosen as a representative for all the families of Paralympians. Best of all, he would be in Beijiing for five days! Our close family friends Barb Pimento and her daughter, Taylor, who is Ceili's godmother, looked after the kids while Eamonn was gone. The kids adore them, and we were so lucky they could all spend that time together. I was still fighting the feelings of guilt for being away from them, but knowing they were with Barb and Taylor eased my mind. Tarabh started kindergarten while I was away, but that just reminded me about my goals for raising my kids: I didn't want to create any kind of weakness for them; I only wanted to bring my kids strength.

My mom was finally going to get to see China, and she and my sister had a great trip planned through Hong Kong and Beijing, culminating in the games. My dad was not up for the trip, but having some family there was a huge boost for me. The only problem in Beijing was that Eamonn was there for only a few days and was not allowed into the athletes' village, and I was not allowed out.

With some help from one of the Chinese volunteers I was able to describe one of the village entrances to Eamonn, and we met just outside the gate and sat on the curb. We had about half an hour together, but it was such a lift for me — it actually gave me energy. I knew that was probably my only chance to see him in Beijing. I wouldn't be able to see him run with the torch, but I hoped to catch it on one of the TVs in the athletes' lounge. He would also attend the Opening Ceremony, but it was unlikely that I would see him there.

Eamonn running with the torch

Before the Opening Ceremony, all the athletes were bused into a secure area where we waited for the start of the parade. We were given bagged lunches with sandwiches, water, and cookies while we waited. It was a very long, very hot wait. We were glad we weren't competing for a few more days because this would not have helped prepare us for racing.

Eamonn texted that he was already inside, sitting way up in the top seats. He said it was about 40 degrees Celsius in there.

As we started to line up for the Athletes' Parade, I got chills. The range of emotions was overwhelming, and my head was swimming. We made our way down a ramp, and I recognized it from the TV. Just a couple of weeks before, I had watched Constantina Diță-Tomescu run down that very ramp as she completed the last lap of her gold medal race.

When we stepped into the Bird's Nest stadium, the atmosphere enveloped me. I was awestruck. I was surrounded by so many noises, colours, and lights, and it was unlike anything you could ever imagine. As I started processing everything, I realized that the stadium was packed to the top — 100,000 people, cheering for and supporting Paralympic Sport. I looked around wide-eyed and saw the sea of athletes in front of me. There were participants from every country imaginable — some I had never even heard of — walking and wheeling proudly. Every one of them was there overcoming obstacles, refusing to give in to their disability, and living life to its fullest. To the left of us were hundreds of volunteers dancing with scarves, welcoming us to the Games. In a way, I was glad I could see only 3 percent of this. I don't think I would have been able to take it all in. The whole experience made me think about where I had come from to get there. The emotions I felt were indescribable.

We took our seats in a prime location for the ceremony, and Angus curled up under the seat beside me. We were given a bag filled with props that would be used throughout the event — flags, flashlights, bells, they all had a role in the ceremony. We were still looking around in amazement when I heard Meghan shout, "Eamonn!" and A.R. started waving. Eamonn, wearing his Canadian torchbearer shirt, had made it past security and was heading toward us.

Because a seat had been left open for Angus, Eamonn had a place to sit, and we were able to be together to watch the Opening Ceremony. This was definitely a once-in-a-lifetime memory for me, and being able to share it with Eamonn made it perfect.

The ceremony was inspiring beyond words. One of the first performers was a Chinese singer who was blind. He sang a powerful ballad in Chinese, then told the audience if he were able to have his sight back, there were only three things he would truly want to see: his mom, his dad, and all of us.

The singer was followed by a young girl in a wheelchair. She had been injured in the Sichuan earthquake earlier that year. It had been her dream to perform with the Chinese National Ballet. Suddenly she was surrounded by ballerinas; the National Ballet of China had come to her. They picked her up, and together they performed a beautiful dance to Ravel's *Bolero*; she danced from the waist up, and the ballet company became her legs. It brought tears to the eyes of everyone watching. The next performers were a troupe of Chinese dancers who were hearing-impaired. They danced by feeling the vibrations of the music and did so precisely in time with one another. Another stunning performance. It seemed that each act at the Opening Ceremony built on the last and took me to another level of awe and inspiration.

Finally it came time to light the torch. A Chinese woman entered the stadium, led by her guide dog. She was the first female Paralympic athlete who had won a gold medal for China. She was also the first guide-dog owner in China. She carried the torch around the stadium and passed it on to Hou Bin, a Chinese athlete who uses a wheelchair and specializes in the high jump.

He had a special device that held the torch hooked to the side of his wheelchair. He was directly under the Paralympic cauldron, which was perched at the top of the Bird's Nest, and a rope hung down. Hou took hold of the rope and began to climb, while still in his wheelchair, to the top of the Bird's Nest Stadium. He pulled himself all the way up to the top of the stadium, where he lit the cauldron.

Hou's strength and determination were unbelievable. I could see his silhouette on the big screen in the stadium. He was about three-quarters of the way up when he paused for a moment. You could tell how hard it must have been to keep going, but I could feel his resolve as he pushed through the pain. I burned that image into my mind, and I knew I would call on that mental picture when I needed a push in our race.

The experience had already been life changing. What an honour to be there! But as we left the stadium, we switched gears. It was time to get back to our "jobs" and return to thinking about our competition. The next day the real work began.

Our training days continued in the same manner as previously, and before we knew it, it was time to race. Our racing schedule was very different from Munich. We had a heat on Tuesday, then the repechage was on Wednesday, and the final was Thursday. There were no rest days if we went to repechage — all the more reason to win our heat and go straight to the final.

There were some new countries we had never competed against before. China had entered a boat, and so had South Africa. We were not sure what to anticipate, but we did expect big things from China.

Because there were only 12 countries racing, only the first place boats in each heat would go straight to the final. Great Britain was in our heat, so we would have to beat them to make it through. I felt that we could do it, but in my heart, I was afraid of them.

We lined up at the gates. This was it — time to cash in all that extra practice, all those days at the gym with Marvin. It was time to see where everyone stood and what we would have to pull out for the final. Germany was racing in the other heat, and we were expecting them to be in first place for that heat.

"Attention... Row!"

I felt as though we were moving in slow motion. We were in third place off the start. I could hear the disappointment in Laura's voice; we were not dominating the way we thought we would. As our spirits fell, so did our boat speed. Italy was out in front — where had they come from? The race ended much as it had begun: Italy won and went straight through to the final.

We finished in fifth place, followed closely by Brazil. In the other heat, China came in first place, followed by the USA and then Germany. Everything had changed. We had gotten faster, but so had the rest of the world.

On the course in Beijing

The repechage was the next day, and the top two boats from each heat would go on to the final. As we looked at everyone's times, we realized with sinking hearts that there was a chance we wouldn't even make the A Final.

We had a team meeting that night and reviewed all the possible errors and what we could do to improve. Laura went over some new calls, and we all resolved to turn things around. Then Laura said what we were all thinking.

"I didn't come all the way to Beijing to row in the B Final."

As we got into the boat for the repechage the next day, Laura made her way down the boat, giving each of us a goal.

"Scott, power and grace... Tony, bend that oar... Vicky, strong finishes... Meghan, pivot and swing."

We were on a mission. The B Final was not an option.

We raced with new-found strength and passion. We were rowing for our lives and pulling with everything we had on every stroke. We had Germany to contend with, and Brazil was right beside us — they were not giving it away either. We executed our race plan perfectly. Everyone's head was in the right place, and we rowed one of our best races ever. We squeezed in just ahead of Brazil, taking second place to Germany and making the A Final. We were ecstatic. I felt like we had just won gold. We set our sights on a goal, we executed the plan, and we got what we wanted. What a feeling of accomplishment. We felt set for the final the next day. Now we could go in with confidence, knowing exactly what we needed to do to win. We would hear "O Canada" on that podium.

The next afternoon as Laura did her walk down the boat, she had new things to say to everyone, but when she got to me she was stuck for a moment.

"Don't worry," I said, "we've got this."

We shoved off from the dock and made our way to the warm-up area.

After warming up we were called to the starting gates. As I sat waiting in the dark, I heard splashes on either side of me. Laura explained that there were Chinese divers (apparently wearing Speedos) who were snorkelling under our boat to clean off any weeds that might have been caught in the fin.

As usual, the officials addressed each boat. "Canada... United States of America... China... Italy... Great Britain... Germany... Attention... Row!"

We did our start. The first stroke was strong, but then I felt someone miss the water with the next stroke.

"It's okay," I told myself, remembering some sports psychology. "If you have a bad stroke, just do three perfect ones to make up for it."

We could still fix this. Then I felt someone miss another. Okay, it was getting tougher to fix, but it was still possible. The boat lurched again. My heart sank. Laura told us we were in fourth place. There was desperation in her voice as she called to Scott.

"Scott, do it for Yael!" (Yael was his fiancée. Scott sat up and attacked with such force. He was rowing at a stroke rate we had never hit before, but I was having a hard time finding his rhythm. I tried to hear the sounds of the seats sliding up and down, but the sound of the crowd was deafening. The wind was swirling all around me, and I felt utterly confused. I kept rowing, but I could feel that I was out of time with everyone else. We weren't even halfway through the race, and I wanted to quit. It felt horrible. This was not how we rowed; this was a nightmare.

I didn't know where we were in the field, but I knew the reason Laura wasn't telling us was because it was so bad. She was trying to get us back on track, but by now we were all just going through the motions. I knew it was all over, but we had to keep going. In the back of my mind I thought maybe something could still happen to another crew. There might still be hope.

I heard the beeps as the other boats crossed the line, five beeps, and then us. Last place.

I sat there in shock over what had just happened. Italy had come in first place, and Great Britain had placed third. But worst of all, the silver medal belonged to the USA, to the crew we had basically tied a few weeks earlier at the Henley.

We sat in silence for a while. Laura asked us if we wanted to go straight in instead of cooling down. Of course we said yes. I could hear that she was crying. We were called over to the media dock, and we wanted to pretend we didn't hear them, but we knew we had to go. We went and answered their questions about how we felt. That was the hardest interview I've ever had to do. I don't remember what I said — some sort of automatic response about how much the sport was moving forward and how that was a good thing. I couldn't say how I really felt.

We got back in our boat to row back to the dock. I left my goggles off even though I wasn't really allowed to. There was nothing for me to lose now. As we rowed back to the dock, the whole course was spread out in front of me. For the first time, I was able to look around the venue and make out the shadows of the grandstand. The sun was setting, casting a pink glow around us and in front of me. Across Tony's back was the red stripe with CANADA emblazoned in white, stretching back and forth with the rhythm of his stroke. At the same time, I heard the regal sound of the victory music coming from the speakers by the grandstand. I closed my eyes for the comfort of familiar darkness, and tears spilled down my cheeks. It was too much to absorb.

The atmosphere was sombre as we cleaned up and returned to the village. Tony, Meghan, and Scott packed up and left to spend time in China with their families. Eamonn was already back at home with the kids, and I wished I could teleport there, but there was still a week until the Closing Ceremony.

The four and Anne-Renée after the final in Beijing `

Over the week, Laura and I forced ourselves to go to the tourist attractions you're supposed to visit in China — the Great Wall, Tiananmen Square, the Summer Palace, and the Forbidden City. We both just wanted to go home. This was not how I imagined my short career in rowing would end.

CHAPTER 16

We achieve my goal — we cross the 500-metre mark in second place. Germany is behind us, and Great Britain is still ahead. Laura's voice comes over the speaker in a tone I haven't heard before.

"Listen up. I know we can do this, but we have to move together."

I realize what she is actually saying: she can see what is going on, and she knows we can move on Great Britain. Now I have a new goal, and I can't believe it. We could take gold.

Back in Toronto, I heard the same thing over and over. "It's amazing that you went even if you didn't win."

I was so sick of hearing it that I started answering back. "It wasn't amazing. I went there to win." No one seemed to understand. It sounded like I didn't appreciate the opportunity. But rowing was not an opportunity that fell in my lap. I worked hard at it, and I had a goal that I failed to achieve.

Eamonn threw a party for me a few nights after I got back. At the party I was telling Marvin my plans to retire from rowing.

"Now is not the time to quit," he told me. "You don't quit when you are on the bottom. If you're going to quit, quit when you're on top."

I also remember him saying something that made no sense to me at the time: "Sometimes you have to learn how to lose in order to learn how to win." It would be years before I would think back on this and understand what he meant.

But the idea that changed my mind was when he told me that I had a unique opportunity that very few people have a chance to pursue. He didn't mean "opportunity" as a lucky thing; he meant the opportunity to push myself to achieve excellence. He pointed out that I had a whole community supporting me and that they were living through me. When I win, they win, and I had a responsibility to finish this journey.

It wasn't too late. I hadn't won gold in Beijing, but I could start again. I had learned from this experience, and I was going to build on it and push myself even more because that's what elite athletes do.

And right then I was convinced to try again.

Eamonn agreed. There would come a time when I wouldn't be able to do this, and he thought that I should do it while I could.

I didn't realize this at the time, but I really had accomplished my original goal already. I had been all over the media while I was in Beijing, including a close up of me during the Opening Ceremony. The kids had seen me on TV and in newspapers and heard me on the radio. Tarabh, who was five at the time, told everyone that his mom rowed for Team Canada. Even though the kids at his school knew I was blind and saw me using a guide dog, that wasn't my identity. They identified me as a Canadian athlete.

A happy family

One morning my whole family was walking to the park, and as a man passed, he politely said, "Good morning," and kept walking.

Tarabh looked up at me and declared, "He said good morning because he recognized you. You're famous."

That was the moment I realized the impact I had on them and how proud they were of me.

One Monday morning I took Tarabh and Ceili to school to drop them off. Both of their classrooms had articles about me and Angus, and pictures of us all over the walls. What a message this was giving the kids — not just my own but all of them! They were celebrating me and my disability. Caitlin Patterson and the other teachers at the school played such a huge role in shaping Tarabh and Ceili's attitude about me. They instilled the pride in me that I had desperately dreamed of them having. So much had happened in just three years.

Tarabh and Ceili

At my own school, I returned to the usual congratulations from the teachers I ran into in the halls. After morning announcements we were called down to an assembly in the gym. Because I had been away, I had no idea what it was about.

When I got to the gym, the whole school was assembled. They formed a sea of red and white clothing, and everyone was waving Canadian flags and cheering for me. My principal gave a speech about how setting goals and working hard pays off, and she asked me to say a few words to the school. I surprised myself by telling them that sometimes in life it's not about the outcome but about the journey and what you learn on the way. Everywhere I went in the school I would hear "Hi, Ms. Nolan!" Throughout our community, people knew who I was. And I felt like I finally knew who I was.

I was able to move on to new goals. I got back to work with Marvin and was excited to see what a full year of training with him would do for my fitness.

In November, however, during a routine checkup with Dr. Heon, she found a cataract in my left eye that needed to be removed. She referred me to a specialist who was excited to perform the surgery on someone with RP. The specialist told me that because I had such a small amount of vision, the cataract removal would make a world of difference to my vision. It would be clearer and sharper than before, and I would be able to see things at a distance much better. The procedure involved removing the lens of my eye and replacing it with a plastic one. It would mean I couldn't train for four or five days, but I was so excited by the news that my sight would improve. Things had been getting more cloudy and blurry, and I had been scared that I was getting down to my last bit of vision.

In December I went in for the surgery. They gave me some gas to help relax my nerves, and they froze my eye, but I was awake for the whole procedure. The surgical team shone a bright light at my face so I couldn't see anything, and then they cut away the lens of my eye. I blacked out for a few seconds, and when I woke up, they were placing the plastic lens on. I was given eye drops and told that it might be a couple of days before I could see the difference.

I went to sleep that night and looked at the digital clock across from my bed. I was hopeful that maybe in the morning I would be able to read the numbers.

When I woke up the next morning the first thing I did was look at the clock, but it was still blurry. I didn't really expect it to be better overnight. Tomorrow would probably be better.

The next morning was the same. And the next. And the next. In fact, my vision actually seemed worse.

The doctor who did the surgery saw me for a follow-up. She had been extremely kind and friendly before the surgery, but once I told her it was not successful, she seemed cold and dismissive. There was nothing that could be done, so I got on with my life. I admit that I'm glossing over how disappointed I was by the result, but really, what could I do other than get on with things?

Meanwhile, I was having problems with Angus. His interest in other dogs was becoming more of an issue. Jason and I worked together for months to try to fix the problem, but Angus consistently barked and lunged aggressively at other dogs. We finally decided that Angus was not going to change his ways and he needed to be retired. He was given to a lovely family as a pet. It was so hard to say goodbye to him, but as with everything in my life, I was so busy that I just had to keep moving. Angus left on a Wednesday night, and by Thursday morning my new dog arrived.

His replacement was Vegas. Not quite as handsome as Angus, Vegas was a spectacular guide. I didn't realize Angus's limitations until I worked with Vegas.

Of course, he too had his quirks. For one thing, he loved bathtubs. He would hang out in an empty tub when he needed some "alone time," and if he visited a new place, the first thing he did was hop in the bath! The other odd thing about Vegas was that he didn't really like dog food. When I poured his food into his dish, he would ignore it and exhaust every other possibility for people food before he would finally tolerate his own. He would sit patiently beside the kids, waiting for something to drop, he would lick all corners of the kitchen, he would check out the countertops for crumbs, and then he would give in and return to his own bowl.

It took a while to bond with him after having such a strong bond with Angus, but over time we established our own connection. After Jetta had given me the confidence to get back on my feet, Angus gave me the courage to get my life going again, but Vegas inspired diligence and strength to attack my goals. All he needed was a bit of cheese!

Later that season, I got a call from Allison.

"Vicky, I have really bad news," she said. "As you know, Scott has retired. The new athlete who is replacing him is Stu Starkey, and he is a B3."

I knew what that meant. FISA rules stated that you couldn't have two visually impaired athletes in the B3 category, and there was no other man faster than Stu. Since Stu and I were in the same category, the woman I'd had to seat race for my spot in Beijing would automatically get my seat.

I thought fast. There was no way Stu would classify as a B2 because he had too much sight. But I had an appointment with Dr. Heon coming up to check on the cataract situation. My vision was definitely worse than before the surgery, so maybe I would classify as a B2.

Dr. Heon confirmed that I had lost enough vision to put me in the B2 category. A tiny part of me was upset at the decline of my vision, but a much bigger part of me was thrilled that I still had a chance to make the team. I would still have to race for my seat, but at least I had a chance.

While all these things were happening, Eamonn started to function as my manager, promoting my story and contacting various media. I definitely didn't have time to manage all these things and appreciated the support. Pretty soon I had more interviews on TV and on radio shows. You could google my name and find articles about my accomplishments. Tarabh and Ceili really started to believe that their mom was famous, and they told everyone they met that their mom rowed for Canada.

One day the kids saw Eamonn lifting weights at home.

Tarabh asked, "Dad, what are you doing?"

"He's lifting weights so he can be strong like mom," Ceili answered.

Awesome!

The Toronto Licensing Tribunal hearing for the taxicab incident happened in February. The driver was given another chance to admit his mistake, but he did not. The panel asked me how the incident had affected me, and I had the chance to tell them how it had robbed me of my independence and confidence to travel.

After deliberating, they revoked the driver's licence, a landmark decision. A reporter who wrote for the taxicab newspaper was present, and he told us this would send a strong message to the taxi community. That Sunday morning I was on the front page of the *Sun* newspaper with the headline "Blind Woman Sees Justice."

After that, I was invited to speak on John Moore's show on CFRB radio. It was live, and I was in the studio. Other visually impaired people called in to thank me. One university student told me that she had a stranger hail her a cab every day after class because no taxi would stop for her and her dog. It felt good to raise some awareness and to know that this kind of discrimination was happening to others as well. While I understand some people have a discomfort with dogs, I really want people to know that a service dog deserves special consideration. A service dog is not like a pet.

The NART selection camp happened again in June, and I had to race the same woman I'd raced the year before. This time we were in Montreal, and it was just her against me.

For the three days leading up to the races, Laura collected data as we practiced that consistently showed I was faster. My erg scores had consistently been faster as well. But A.R. kept giving reasons why the woman from British Columbia was actually faster: when I rowed she said I had a tail wind, or that Meghan was throwing the rows in my favour. I guess she saw more potential in the new girl, but it was incredibly frustrating for me. Then Meghan injured her back and had to be replaced temporarily. When the new athlete came to fill in, my speeds were still all faster.

Once again, I beat my challenger in seat racing. I was clearly faster than her, but the coach decided she was going to give the woman another chance to come back in July to race me again. I wasn't going to let her beat me. It was more motivation for me to train harder.

Changes were happening at Rowing Canada. There was a new High Performance Director, and he was changing things in Adaptive Rowing. After the seat racing, we met with him. He told us that we'd have to step things up if we wanted to go to the World Championships in Poland. He would not be sending any boats to the Worlds unless they could prove that they had a strong chance at winning a medal. He sounded doubtful that any of the adaptive rowers would be going.

Laura asked him if our boat would be shipped over to Poland with the rest of the National Team gear. He said he was not sending us a boat until we showed him the time he wanted to see. The container was leaving the following week, on the day of our time trial, so we wouldn't be having our boat shipped over. If we pulled the right time, we would have to rent a boat in Europe. Laura told him in no uncertain terms that we would be going to Poland. Failure was not a possibility to us. He still seemed skeptical.

We pulled an acceptable time on the time trial, but it was close to the borderline, so the director wanted us to pull another one in a month. It had to be significantly better for his approval. None of the other adaptive boats made the time standard, and they were not approved to compete. We were frustrated, but we accepted the challenge. Plus I still had to win another seat race; that and the director's push for a faster time motivated me to train hard.

There was a bike-riding fundraiser for the Foundation Fighting Blindness, a 140-kilometre bike ride from Toronto to Collingwood. I was asked to join because of my Paralympic status, and I agreed. Typically, visually impaired riders pair up with a sighted partner and ride a tandem bike. Eamonn and I had always talked of trying a tandem but had never gotten around to it. It would be additional training and it was an important cause. The spin classes I did to train were very tough, but they whipped my cardio fitness into shape. Between spin class, my rowing training, and Marvin's workouts, things were going well.

I never thought I'd ride a bike again

At our camp in July, I beat the other athlete again and finally put an end to the seat racing. At the time trial we raced at 94 percent of the gold medal standard, which was good enough to go to Poland. But once again the director put us off, telling us he needed time to consider it. I realized that this could really be the end of my rowing career and of Canada's Adaptive Rowing Team.

In the meantime, Eamonn wanted to go to Ireland with the kids to visit his mom. He really wanted me to come with him, and it was just for two weeks. It had been a few years since I had last visited my mother-in-law, and I wasn't sure what the right move was. There was a chance the director would say no to Poland, in which case I didn't wanted to miss spending that time with my family. Also, if I kept rowing through to 2012, this would definitely be the last summer I could leave for a while.

After weighing all the factors, I saw no reason why I couldn't train in Ireland the same way I did in Toronto. I had a connection to a rowing club in Limerick, and there was a gym with an erg. I decided to go.

In Ireland, my motivation was higher than ever. When I got back, I wanted everyone to notice how hard I had worked while I was away. A young woman who was on the Irish Junior National Team at the Athlunkard Boat Club offered to go out with me, and I rowed with her in a double on the River Shannon.

I also went to the gym every day and practiced on an erg. They had a different type of rowing machine than I usually used, one that simulated a headwind. There was more tension as you pulled back, and you really had to control the glide forward and not rush it. It helped with the primary focus I had for those two weeks — developing a stronger rhythm. I had to learn to drive faster and glide up to the catch. The rowing stroke can be thought of as having two parts: the drive and the recovery. The drive is the backward motion as you push the legs down and pull the oar to your chest. The recovery is a controlled, steady glide back up to the front of the boat. On the glide up, you let the speed of the boat run under you, and it can't be rushed. The nature of this machine forced me to really work on that with strong drive and rhythm around the finish. Every day, I thought about swinging out and gliiiiiiiding up to the catch, and gradually it got easier and more automatic.

I even added a third workout in Ireland and went running each day with Eamonn to keep up my cardio fitness.

On my fourth day in Ireland, I got the email: we were going to Poland. I would have only one day to get ready when I got back home.

I was happy to be going to the World Championships, but there were some alarming changes. Allison had been laid off, and A.R. was not going to be coaching us over the summer because she was coaching the Quebec Team for the Canada Summer Games that year. Rowing Canada was giving us a one-week camp in St. Catharines with two different coaches, and then the five of us would fly to Poland on our own. Another National Team coach would coach us for the ten days we were there. As soon as our race was over, we would be flown out of Poland before the end of the regatta. And they were charging us a fee of $1,000 to attend.

Meghan and me in St. Catharines (Canadian rowers who have won medals have their names engraved in the sidewalk)

We really seemed to be taking steps backward and starting from scratch. If we were going to succeed, we needed more coaching, more time together, and more support. I felt like they were writing us off and didn't know what we were capable of. We wanted the same support that the able-bodied team had.

Most of all, we wanted respect. Of course we knew we had to earn it, but it was one of those cycles: you can't earn the medals without the support, and you can't get support without the medals. But honestly, each of these challenges we faced just pumped us up even more. We wanted to prove to everyone that we had the discipline, commitment, and ability to succeed.

I was anxious to show my team how much I had developed while I was away. All my efforts really paid off. After the first row, everyone commented on my progress and on how much better things felt. I was thrilled that they could tell how hard I had worked, and I couldn't wait to see the results in a race.

Our trip to Poland was short and uneventful. As in Munich, we were pretty much ignored by most of the rest of the Canadian Team. A couple of people would sit with us at meals; Al Morrow was always supportive and friendly, and a handful of the AB rowers would make the effort to talk to us. As for the rest, it actually seemed as though they were trying to avoid us. The atmosphere it created didn't feel like indifference — it was more like they felt they were above us. We knew that many of them thought we didn't belong there with them. I think it was because we didn't have to live at a training centre, and we got to train from home for most of the year. They believed we weren't working as hard as them. I'm not really sure what the reason was, and I didn't really take it personally until one occasion when we overheard one of the women complaining about her accreditation photo.

"I look like an adaptive rower." She laughed, and the men around her laughed too.

None of us spoke up. I can't really explain why. As much as we didn't want to be treated as outsiders, we knew we were. These athletes had been part of the program for longer than us, and they worked closely with all of the staff who were there. We didn't even have a coach with us. We were on our own, and we figured keeping our heads down and staying focused on the race would be the best way to go. It boiled my blood to be looked down on. I hadn't put in the hours year-round at a training centre that she had, but I had spent a lifetime overcoming hardship and discrimination. I had risen above it — we all had — and I thought we deserved respect for that.

We made the A final and came in fourth place just behind Germany. Great Britain was back in first place, and Italy won silver.

Our director met us after the race and gave us a stern speech about how we didn't perform up to expectations. He had the nerve to tell us that we didn't really race. I was glad when Meghan pointed out that we didn't do this for a trip to Poland. She told him we were serious and committed, and we needed more from Rowing Canada in order to perform.

The director admitted that he had not fully understood what Adaptive Rowing was until he saw the races, and that he was confident we could be on top with the right coaching and support. He was willing to invest in us and help us get on the podium, but we had to start producing faster times.

We left Poland feeling okay with the result. Our team had been given only a few weeks to train together; we all knew what we could accomplish with more.

CHAPTER 17

I have to make it hurt even more. I am seeing stars, and I know I'm entering a whole new level of fatigue. This pain is no longer a good pain — this is a nightmare that's not going to end for another 400 metres! But I have come this far, and this is where it counts. That first 600 metres will be wasted if I don't hold it together now.

Rowing Canada decided to hire a lead coach for the Adaptive Program who would work full-time and oversee the whole program. This person would also act as the coach for our LTA4+ boat. Rowing Canada would also allocate more money for more camps together, and the Adaptive Team would work more closely with the Women's Team.

Over the winter we started a team weightlifting program set up by A.R. that set out exercises specifically designed for rowers. I found it really motivating and liked the focus it brought. In

December, our coach asked us to set three goals for the new year. I sent mine out to everyone in an email, and once I had told everyone, I was committed to seeing my intentions through. I wanted to achieve the following:

- Be on the podium in 2010.
- Build noticeably stronger arms.
- Develop quicker catches.

I started weightlifting at school as well as with Marvin. I would train with my students, setting goals with them and teaching them about my training regime. It was great for me, but it also ended up helping some of the more troubled kids in my class by giving them something to work toward too.

My arms were becoming more defined, and I noticed that it was becoming harder to fit some shirts over my biceps. Jeans that fit were also hard to find as my quad muscles got bigger. I started working with a nutritionist and changed my diet to include much more protein and more vegetables and fruit. I worked even harder on my erg workouts, particularly in trying to master the catch part of the stroke and visualizing how it would transfer on the water. With each of my workouts, I made sure that I pushed myself harder than the last time.

In February I entered the indoor erg contest in the 2,000 metre category. I'd had a goal time in mind for months, but as the competition date got closer, I reduced my goal time by 5 seconds. I knew my splits had really been dropping with all the work I was putting in.

I remembered the year before when I had raced a new woman in my category. I had heard what her best time was and what she was hoping to get that year. Her goal had been much slower than what I was aiming for that year, so instead of pushing myself as hard as I could go, I just made sure I was faster than she was.

I had a whole new attitude this year even though I was racing her again. I imagined I was up against Great Britain and Germany, and I pushed myself through each part of the race, imagining them right there beside me. Laura had come for support, and she was shouting calls to me from the stands. I was totally focused and determined to hit my goal. I felt strong, and I felt confident. I finished with a time 1 second faster than my goal, and I knew with more training I could do even better.

Meanwhile I continued to do radio and print interviews, and Tarabh, who was seven by then, talked more and more about his mom being famous. I was asked to do a speech at his school about Beijing, and we auctioned off some Beijing souvenirs. The skill-testing question for the auction was "Whose mom competed in the Beijing Games?" Tarabh and Ceili became well-known by all the kids in the school and often witnessed the older kids stopping me to ask me questions and even asking for my autograph!

For Chinese New Year, Tarabh's class had to write fortunes to put in cookies, and Tarabh wrote, "One day your mom will be famous like mine."

Rowing Canada planned our first NART camp to be in Tennessee with the Canadian Women's Team. The plan was for us to train alongside them to develop competitive skills and work on how to push through a boat when racing. It was a two-week camp in March, and luckily my new principal, Andrew McLachlan, was as supportive as the principal who had hired me. He approved my leave, and although I lost two weeks' pay, my class was looked after by a supply teacher.

Our team did not do well rowing alongside the women. They were beating us on all the pieces (the parts of the workout that have specific rates or focuses). Even alongside a single scull we were battling it out. I wanted to be able to hold our own against a pair or double one day. It seemed like a reasonable goal to have. A strong pair or a double can be similar in speed to a four. Even though they have only two rowers, the boats are lighter and they don't have to carry the weight of a coxswain. A double is typically quicker than a pair because the rowers each have two oars instead of one. But even though we didn't feel highly successful against those boats, we definitely felt like we were learning from the Women's Team, and it was valuable time together.

After that camp, two big changes put things in high gear. First, the new lead coach, Jeff Dunbrack, started his job. He was new to Rowing Canada and brought with him a strong background in rowing. He had the also worked with the Canadian Wheelchair Basketball Team and was very knowledgeable about both the Paralympics and athletes with disabilities.

The second change was that Stu, the man who had replaced Scott in Poland, had to quit, and we needed a new male athlete for our boat. Fortunately, Jeff had been actively looking for new athletes. Quite by accident, he discovered a man who qualified as a Paralympic athlete but had been rowing as an able-bodied athlete for the last four years. His name was David, and we learned that he had albinism that caused vision loss. We met him at the next camp at the Training Centre in London, Ontario. We began a week-long camp to get some more competitive experience training with the women. The Adaptive Team had a few days on our own to try rowing as a crew and to get used to having David in our boat, and then we did pieces with the pairs and doubles. We were expected to row at a similar speed to the AB pairs and doubles, and there were other configurations — singles, pairs — that should have been slower than we were.

The workout was set up so that we were paired with another boat for a 2,000-metre distance. The winner went on to race a winner from another pairing, and the loser went on to race another boat that had lost. By the end of the workout, one boat would come out on top.

We lost our first piece, and it just kept going downhill from there. After the first few pairings, I wanted the pieces to end, I just didn't want to do anymore, and I felt defeated. We lost against every boat, including the singles and the new athletes on the team. It was humiliating and embarrassing, much like the very first rowing camp I ever attended. It was the feeling I'd sworn I never wanted to feel again. Like in Montreal. I was giving in to negative feelings and not fighting hard the way I knew I should.

I had to change my attitude more than I needed to improve my fitness. I had to find a way to attack in those situations. I needed to find the drive to push through other crews and the confidence to know it could be done. I wanted to be an athlete who would not back away from a challenge. I remembered the director telling us that had been our failing in Poland: crews moved on us, and we didn't push back. I needed to learn how to do that.

Jeff increased our practice schedule to three a day instead of two. I didn't think this would last very long; I was sure we couldn't keep up with that regime. But I was wrong, we handled it, and we got fitter, even during those two weeks.

Jeff broke the rowing stroke down from start to finish, and that extra workout, which was always a technical practice, helped us work on small details. He started teaching us how to be aggressive and how to push back when crews were moving on us. He told us that it was going to hurt, but we had to push past what we thought were our limits and test out what was possible. Feeling comfortable rowing was a sign that we were not pushing limits — we should always be pushing beyond the comfort zone. As we worked on that, things started coming together.

The next time we went out with the women, we were starting to hold our own against some of the crews. The new approach was to be confident and to calmly move the boat together. When Laura told us to focus on a specific part of the stroke, rather than panicking and attacking without thinking, we thought about being stealthy and composed and executing the plan that she had. It worked. Once we experienced the feeling of inching up on a boat and moving through it seat by seat — once we knew it was possible — we did it more and more often and we started to realize that we could achieve incredible results. By the end of the camp we were keeping up with the top double that was going to compete in the World Cup later that month. They became our new training partners.

During the next few camps in St. Catharines, we learned that Jeff really took initiative and thought outside the box to find us as many competitive opportunities as possible. Sometimes it meant doing our training session beside a boys' crew or racing against able-bodied rowers in masters' events.

The first time we "picked a fight" was with a men's flyweight crew. We should have been able to go faster than their boat. The workout was four ten-minute pieces, and they plowed right through us on every single one. It was demoralizing for us to lose every piece, but Jeff talked to us afterwards and explained that those boys were hauling on their oars with every single stroke. They gave 100 percent to every moment, even on the low-rate parts of the workout that fell between the ten-minute pieces. He told us that sometimes we looked casual, as if we were out for a Sunday paddle. From then on we changed how we rowed, even when we were not in a piece.

The next crew we went out with was a senior women's four, a category for women aged 20 to 25. Their coach asked us if we wanted a head start. This only fired us up more, and of course Jeff said no. After the talk the day before and with our new way of rowing, we demolished the women's four and moved on to a men's four.

We met with the men at a masters' race at the Central Ontario Rowing Association (CORA) regatta in St. Catharines. We were racing masters men aged 25 to 35. There were six boats in the race. We were not eligible for any medals, but we did it for the experience. We went out and rowed hard, overtaking boats, fighting back and forth with others. It was a great race, and in the end we finished in second place, just 1 second behind the first-place boat. We were starting to turn heads and earn respect. More crews started asking to train with us.

In August we had a month-long camp. We had never been together for that long a stretch, and we had already had five weeks of camps since January. Our training program was definitely more demanding than ever before.

Camp was extremely difficult on me this time. Eamonn took the kids to Ireland for a visit, so I didn't even get to see them on weekends. We were living in a dorm at Brock University, and there was nowhere to go within walking distance. It was a really, really long haul. The four of us (Tony, David, Meghan, and I) shared a townhouse and a vehicle, so we had to do everything together. Laura lived in St. Catharines, so she had her own place to retire to at the end of each long day. The whole experience was exhausting — physically, mentally, and emotionally. I had a calendar on my desk, and I crossed off the days, counting down until I got to go home again.

Even the rowing itself was long and hard, and our progress seemed at a standstill. We didn't really seem to be getting any faster. We were even having trouble hitting some of the rates we had wanted. There were many, many days that I asked myself why I was putting myself through this. If all this insane work didn't get us to the podium, then I was ready to quit.

In September I went home for two weeks, and Meghan decided to stay in Toronto and train with me in a pair. I considered her my family by then, and it was great to have her around with Eamonn and the kids. The World Masters Rowing Championships were happening in St. Catharines that year, and we decided to enter the event for able-bodied women aged 25 to 35. We had no idea how we would do, but we wanted the experience. And, truth be told, we wanted gold.

We trained together at Bayside Rowing Club, close to my house, with the support of Dominic Kahn, the head coach at Bayside. He had some radical ideas and was extremely passionate about rowing. You had no choice but to get excited about the sport when you heard his metaphors and his teaching.

The day of the race, Eamonn was out in the stands watching for us as the race came down. I had told him that because we were a composite crew, I would be wearing the purple Bayside unisuit and Meghan would be wearing her Winnipeg unisuit. He saw a purple unisuit in second place, and his heart sank. A pair in white T-shirts was out in front, and he thought they looked too good for the event. They were ahead of everyone and starting to get open water. They moved so well together and made it all look easy. He was hoping that the boat in front was rowed by ex-Olympians so that at least our loss would be justified and we wouldn't be too upset. Also, it was an able-bodied event, so our finishing second was not unthinkable.

As Meghan and I crossed the finish line, we were close enough to the grandstand for Eamonn to realize that the boat in front was us! At the last minute we had found out we were required to wear matching uniforms, so we threw on white shirts. We were the crew that pushed through everyone else and pulled the fastest time in our division. We were surprised and so happy. It was another step toward our goal checked off. We were awarded our gold medals at the dock where the USA had been presented the Henley gold just two years earlier, and I wondered if there would be another medal in our future.

Me and Meghan after winning the World Masters Rowing Championships

My principal and the Toronto District School Board continued to support my training. I am still so grateful for their support; it was in sharp contrast to the treatment I had received previously. In mid-September my team returned for another ten-day camp with a time trial at the end. This time trial was for the entire Canadian Team and would determine which boats would go to New Zealand for the World Championships that year.

As we prepared for the time trial, things really started to improve. We even pulled 03:20 a couple of times, which was faster than Great Britain's gold medal time of 03:25 from the year before, and also the current world record. But I assumed that GB was pulling 03:15 by then, and I wanted more speed. There was no room for complacency.

More of the able-bodied rowers were starting to talk to us, especially since we were often training together. The women would sit with us at breakfast and joke with us on the dock. Sarah Bonikowsky interviewed the team as she was studying occupational therapy and integrating children with disabilities into sports. In general, the Adaptive Team was much more fit than it had been, and that also helped me to feel like I belonged.

After our time trial, we received many nods of approval from the able-bodied team coaches and high performance staff. They were impressed with our technique and our speed. We were the best they had seen in adaptive rowing, and many of them congratulated us.

When the percentages were posted, we had the highest percentage of all the boats — 98 percent! There were still some athletes who looked down on us — "Yeah, but it's *adaptive* rowing" — but there were also many who seemed genuinely happy for us. Gaining respect was a slow process, but we were earning it.

As the competition drew nearer, we were invited to train against one of the women's boats, just the two boats side by side. One of the women seemed totally unimpressed that she had to row with us. She did not communicate with Laura to make the pieces run smoother. Rather than trying to stay next to each other, which would force both crews to work harder, she seemed to take every opportunity to get away from us so that each boat ended up doing its own workout. It was frustrating, but we persevered, and the times that we were beside each other, we pushed hard.

Sometimes we came out on top, and sometimes they did, but what I learned also applied to my life beyond rowing: It can take a while to push through a crew or overcome a challenge. But if you chip away at it inch by inch with perseverance, you will get through it.

CHAPTER 18

With less than 400 metres to go, Great Britain is right beside us. We are in second place by inches. We are moving so well together in our boat, riding the edge of control, but I'm not thinking about that.

"In two, we're going to swing like the lightweight double!" Laura commanded.

I loved this move. I could feel the speed pick up when we did it right. I took a second to compose myself and to feel the rest of the crew. Then we put the move into action, swinging to full length and feeling the boat glide out from under us.

It was working! Even before Laura told us, I could feel that we were moving faster.

Our last camp flew by, and then it was time to go. We were flying to Victoria first, training for a week, and then flying from there to New Zealand.

As I knew from past team travels, taking a guide dog on an airplane is quite an experience. A lot of thought and planning must go into the journey beforehand. The fact that this would be the longest flight I had ever been on made it that much more stressful. The distance to Beijing was nothing compared to this flight!

Step one was researching New Zealand's laws about importing service animals. Fortunately, the event's organizing committee emailed Rowing Canada a webpage that had the rules and documentation I needed. Eamonn went to our vet and got the necessary paperwork. I completed and signed a bio-inspection declaration and collected all of Vegas's guide-dog school certification. Eamonn made several phone calls to the Customs department at Auckland Airport, and Rowing Canada faxed all the documentation ahead of time. I bought a large bag of Vegas's food to take with me even though it was very heavy and greatly restricted what I could bring for myself. I also packed his bowls and toys.

The night before our flight I fed him only half his dinner, and the morning of the flight he got only a handful of food and a little water. Although I have had good experiences in the past, I am always stressed out wondering how the airline staff will react to having a dog on board. Air New Zealand had asked me to sign a declaration that Vegas would not accidentally urinate on the flight, so I was even more anxious than usual about our trip.

As we were loading the car for the airport, my phone rang. I couldn't believe what I heard on the other end. Biosecurity New Zealand was calling to inform me that a specific blood test was missing from my package of documentation for Vegas. The information and checklist I had been given did not mention this blood test, but there was no way around this problem. The blood test had to be done six months before travel, and Vegas would not be admitted without the test. If I tried to bring him, he would be shipped back to Canada in cargo at my expense.

I tried to stay composed and deal with the situation, but I couldn't speak without my voice cracking. I knew I couldn't bring him, but what was I going to do with him? My flight was leaving in three hours, and I was a five-hour flight away from home. I wasn't even thinking ahead about how I would manage without him; I was only thinking about leaving him on his own.

Vegas, of course, had no idea what was going on. It was hard to look at him, so oblivious as he rested his chin on my arm. I could imagine his big eyes looking up at me, hopeful that I would need him to take me somewhere. He nuzzled my arm, and I broke down. He was such a faithful companion; as long as he was helping me, he was happy. How could I walk away from him in a strange city, leave him with strangers, and fly to the other side of the world? I was beside myself.

We arrived at the Victoria Airport, and Michelle, one of Rowing Canada's administrators, met me at the door. She had arranged for me to take the last possible flight over to Vancouver to catch the New Zealand flight — buying me a few more minutes with Vegas. And she had a possible solution.

Michelle was flying to Toronto in three days, and she was willing to keep Vegas and bring him to Toronto to meet Eamonn. She had a dog of her own and a big yard for him to run around in, and Vegas knew her. I was still upset, but there was so much relief in knowing I was leaving him with someone who would care for him. I couldn't stand to think of him worrying about me. At least back in Toronto he would have some comforts.

I pulled his dog food and his toys out of my suitcase, and together, Michelle and I made a list of what he needed, and I gave Vegas a pat on the head and hugged him around the neck. He thought it was a game and put his paws up on my shoulders. I turned my back and walked away from him, trying to get it over with quickly. He tried to follow, and Michelle pulled him back.

He started whining and struggled to come after me. I could hear his paws slipping on the shiny floor as he scrambled. It's as though he were saying, "Hold on, you forgot me!" I couldn't look back.

Meghan was walking with me. "Don't start crying," she said, "or I'll start."

The two of us were wiping away tears as we went through security and crossed out of his sight. I had my cane with me, and Meghan and Laura were always great at helping me to get around. I managed better with Vegas, of course, but my brain automatically flipped to coping mode. I could find a way to cope as long as Vegas could.

I knew I had to stay focused on my goal, and I was going to see this through. My resolve to get on the podium was even stronger. Over the last four years I had trained my muscles to be stronger, but for more than ten years I had been strengthening my spirit in the challenges I had faced and the battles I had fought. There had been some dark, dismal times, but I had moved on from them with more clarity and vision than I had ever had before.

When I talked to Eamonn, he told me that after all this I had better get a gold medal and make this personal tragedy worthwhile. I agreed, but I was scared — deep down, I didn't think we could do it.

I was in the lounge when I heard an announcement: "Paging passenger Victoria Nolan to check in." A little surprised, I collected my things, and Meghan helped me up to the check-in desk.

"Oh. Hello, Victoria. Where is your dog?" the concierge sounded so disappointed. I explained the situation, and he was very sorry to hear it. He had prepared treats for Vegas and had supplies ready in case Vegas had to relieve himself. Even if Vegas weren't with me, it helped ease my mind to know that the airline was supportive.

The concierge arranged for the passenger next to me to help me out if necessary, but there was no need. At least five cabin crew members visited with me as we were waiting to take off. They explained the safety procedures and let me feel the life-jacket toggles and the oxygen mask. They went through how the entertainment system worked and practiced it with me several times. They checked on me frequently throughout the flight and anticipated every possible need I might have. Once again, those kindnesses had a large impact on rebuilding my self-esteem. In a world where I am often not considered, special treatment mends some of the hurt and offers a temporary break from the pain of loss. We arrived in Auckland after 14 hours in the air, and despite the duration, it was a surprisingly pleasant flight.

The organizing committee was at the airport to meet us. One of the coordinators greeted me with a big smile and said she was sorry about Vegas. I told her it was not okay. I wanted them to know that having Vegas taken away left me shuffling around in the dark. He brought mobility and independence to my life. He helped me to have my freedom.

I was advised by Rowing Canada to keep quiet about the whole thing. They thought it would detract from the regatta, and they wanted me to stay focused. I knew that they just didn't want to look responsible for the situation, but I also knew I couldn't handle the stress and drama of a media circus. I kept quiet.

After another five hours of travelling from the airport in Auckland, we pulled up to our hotel in Wanganui, New Zealand, where we would train for two weeks before heading to the venue. Meghan and I were given one of the motel-type rooms that were accessed from outside the building. They may as well have built me a maze to get to our room, and I wondered if I would ever make sense of how to get around. Meghan was a lifesaver, looking out for me and helping me figure things out. It was a good thing we got along, because I stuck to her like glue!

When we went to the dining hall for lunch, we met up with some of the Women's Team, who had arrived the day before us. We were told that they had not been on the water yet as it was forbidden to touch the water until a Maori blessing had been received. The Maori people of Wanganui had prepared a welcome ceremony for us, and we were not allowed to row on the Waikato River until we had made peace with the water spirits, or *taniwha*.

The entire Canadian Rowing Team, about 70 of us, travelled to the waterfront park and gathered at the entrance. All the men were to assemble in the front, and the women behind them — so the men could protect us. A group of Maori people began to do the *Haka*, which I had been excited to witness, but between my narrow vision and the rows of six-foot-something men, I couldn't see anything. I could hear their aggressive shouts and the stomping of their feet, but I knew I had never seen anything comparable that I could draw from and imagine. I hoped that I could watch someone's video afterward to get a better sense of it.

Fortunately, what followed was interactive and it made up for what I was not able to see.

A Maori custom, once peace was established with new visitors, was to touch noses with each guest to symbolize that we are all one, breathing the same air. There were about 30 Maori people of all ages lined up to welcome us, and we moved along the line touching noses with every person. I was so nervous; I had no depth perception, so if I was not careful, I would either knock foreheads or end up accidentally kissing someone! The Maori people were so friendly and welcoming: along with touching noses, many of them gave us a kiss on the cheek and said "*Kia ora*," which means "welcome."

Maori men about to start the Haka

There were more parts to the ceremony, including storytelling in their longhouse and a ceremonial launching of a war canoe that included four of our rowers in the boat. This was no tourist attraction; we were experiencing real Maori culture.

Once we had made peace with the *taniwha*, or water spirits, we wasted no time getting out on the water. We were based at the Aramoho Wanganui Rowing Club. All our boats had been shipped there, and they were waiting for us when we arrived. It was also pointed out that there was a Canadian flag perched on top of the boathouse. Pat, the club manager, explained that he had to put it up early each morning and take it down each night, otherwise someone would "nick" it.

Our boat was a brilliant red, so bright and vibrant that it cheered me up each time that I saw it. The usual white boats generally blended into the background of the concrete floors and buildings around it, but this red was so striking it was easy to look at. However, our rack was in a difficult spot in the boathouse; it was a little lower than shoulder height, and there were boats both above and below it.

If you watched able-bodied athletes getting their boats, it looked easy. They slid the boat off the rack, put it on their shoulders with one hand, grabbed their oars with the other, and walked it all down to the dock. For us, it was much more involved. I couldn't see much in the boathouse because it was so dark and crowded, and the place was a minefield of obstacles from floor to ceiling. Boats were stacked throughout with riggers jutting out at different heights and locations. There were often oars left on the floor and people coming and going with equipment. The fact that a bump or a scratch to a boat can cause massive damage added to the difficulty. It was the coxswain's job to direct the athletes safely down to the dock, but Laura had the added responsibility of making sure her visually impaired athletes were aware of everything in their path. Communication needed to be precise and efficient, and collecting our gear was usually done under a lot of stress and time constraints.

Laura did a great job, but even still there were accidents. On one occasion, as we lowered one side of the boat and tried to shimmy through all the obstacles, I walked face first into an oarlock. It hit the bridge of my nose initially, but then I felt a sting on my forehead. We were halfway out of the boathouse and the boat was heavy, so I told them I was okay to get down to the dock and we didn't stop. The ramp down to the dock was steep, and Tony had a difficult time keeping his balance. When we put it down, I touched my forehead and felt a bump forming. Laura told me there was a little cut.

The dock was so tiny that there was barely enough room for our boat to fit alongside it. The dock was so small, in fact, that the ramp blocked my oar from sitting flat on the dock. The result was that every time we got ready to push off, my oar was pulled over to the opposite side of the boat, making my seat feel unbalanced and forcing me to sit very far forward. While wearing my blackout goggles, I already felt unstable and nervous. This extra issue made me unsure of what to do until we pushed off and I was able to push my blade out. I hated the adjustment period whenever I went to a new place. But as we pushed off the dock and got moving, it all melted away and I was drawn into the rhythm of the boat: the "plunk" of the blade as it dropped into the water; the "whoosh" of the oar as I pulled it through the waves; and the spinning of the wheels as I glided up to take the next stroke. I fought the feelings of despair because I knew from experience that I would get used to everything after a while.

As we rowed up the Wanganui River, I heard excited gasps and exclamations at how beautiful the scenery was, and my hatred for the blackout goggles returned. Apparently there was a hillside dotted with hundreds of sheep. We were passing houses with beautiful flower gardens. I imagined everything, but it was not the same.

Later on Jeff let me take off the goggles for a bit and I was delighted, but my joy didn't last for long when I realized I couldn't see the banks of the river anyway. We were too far away, and the colours were all blending together. I focused on the smells in the air. People had their fireplaces burning, and it reminded me of the turf fires in Ireland. That cheered me up. It was a cozy reminder of Eamonn, and I decided to enjoy that aspect of the river.

Tarabh and Ceili were now at the age where they were able to articulate how much they missed me, and it was heart-wrenching when they told me this over the phone. Ceili told me that her heart hurt when I was away. I asked them if I should quit rowing so I could stay home with them, and they both emphatically said no, and that they just missed me. Tarabh told me he wanted me to win a gold medal. I swallowed hard. I wanted to win a medal for them — but gold? I tried to think of some inspiring things to say when we didn't get it. I hated to think of them feeling that I had failed. I tried to tell Tarabh that any medal would be awesome, since we were in fourth place last year.

"Yeah, but gold is the best," he said.

Training went really well in Wanganui. We pulled some fast times and dealt with severe wind, current, and waves. By the end of our time there, we felt ready for anything.

My most memorable moment was when we raced our training partners, the lightweight double, for a time trial. We completed the warm-up, but things felt off: my oar was sometimes in too deep, sometimes not deep enough. Then I started to lose my balance as the boat dipped from side to side. The wind was picking up, and the waves were growing in height. We realized how rough it really was after turning the boat and trying to row into the wind. The wind held us back with such force that there were times when our boat was not moving at all. We finished our warm-up anyway and went to the start line.

We sat waiting to hear if we would even continue the piece, fairly certain that we would. It was very rare that a practice was ever cancelled, and generally only if there was lightning. We lined up with the double, heard the start called — "Sit ready, attention, row!" — and we went. We were trying to prove to everyone how hard we had been working all summer and how much we deserved to be there. We were bow ball to bow ball with the double. We pulled ahead for a few strokes, then they pulled ahead. I was feeling good about what we had done so far and was getting ready for our finish. All of a sudden, the double slipped into another gear, and they jumped out in front and finished first. Our time was awesome, however, and we held on to the highest percentage.

By this time, the wind had really picked up speed, and the coaches were calling us to bring the boats in quickly. One of the pairs actually flipped over, and others were filling with water. Our ability to maintain our balance in these conditions gave us confidence that we would be able to row well in anything. Jeff was happy, and we were all feeling really good about our performance. We met afterward and discussed what had gone well and what we still needed to work on. We all agreed that in our last 250 strokes, we needed to be able to turn on the speed the way the double could. Laura had noticed that at the point where they took off, they had made a call for more swing with their bodies. This gave them a longer stroke through the water, and they were able to increase their speed with power. We added "swing like the lightweight double" to our race plan. With that, our time in Wanganui was done, and the whole team departed on a tour bus for Karapiro, an hour away. The World Championships were about to begin.

CHAPTER 19

Any second now, Laura is going to call for the sprint. In the past it was tempting to ease off here to prepare for the painful finish that is about to kick in, but I know now that it's time to pull even harder. Get ready — we're going up.

Once again the Canadian Team took over an entire hotel, this time in Hamilton, about 40 minutes away from the rowing venue. It was a beautiful hotel in the city, close to restaurants and shops. The rooms were huge and filled with light. Our windows were about 10 feet tall, and the ceilings felt so high they must have been 12 feet. Despite not having Vegas there to guide me, all the space and light helped me adjust quickly to my surroundings.

The venue was well-organized and spread out, so I also got my bearings there pretty quickly. As usual, I didn't get to see the course because I always had to have my goggles on, but I was in full-focus mode anyway. I wanted to do whatever it took to be on the podium.

The weather was a bit of a problem; New Zealand was just coming out of winter and was dealing with strong winds. The course was often closed due to the weather conditions, so there were many times when athletes could not get on the water to practice and could only work out on an erg. This happened to us once, but on another day we managed to get our row in before they closed the course.

Two days before our heat, we were waiting at the bus stop at 7:00 a.m. when we got a phone call that the course was closed again. We were starting to panic. I remember when we were in Munich I would have welcomed a delay or a reason not to row. But in New Zealand, with my strong new focus and drive, I was dying to get out and race. I couldn't sit around all day waiting. At least we knew that all the other crews were in the exact same situation, but it still didn't feel good.

Then Jeff had a brilliant idea. The boat we were renting to race in was from the Wakapita River Boat Club, which was within walking distance from our hotel. Jeff phoned them and asked if we could borrow another boat and train on their river, and they said yes. It wasn't much of a workout — the river had a ridiculously fast current — but getting out on the water gave us an advantage over every other crew and kept us on track and focused. We felt more confident.

The night before our heat I met with Laura to go over the race plan. We hadn't done this since Munich, and I thought it was a good idea. She asked me what I wanted to accomplish in this heat. I wasn't expecting that question, and I had to think about it for a moment. Great Britain was not in our heat, but we had Germany, Ukraine, Poland, Ireland, and USA. The top two countries would go straight to the final, and I was pretty sure that would easily be us and Germany, so making the final wasn't much of a goal.

I said what I would honestly have loved to come true: "I want to scare Great Britain. I want to pull a faster time than they pull in their heat and really surprise them."

When I started saying it, it was a lofty goal, but as I heard myself say it out loud I started to believe it was a possibility. It scared me a little because having that as a goal meant I had to try to make it happen, and the possibility of failure is always scary.

As we sat in the boat on our way out to race the heat, Jeff told us he wanted us to place first. He told us that even if we were safely in second place, we were to keep going and push it all the way down to the finish line. That was our plan anyway, but I got excited hearing that confidence from Jeff.

We were tied with Germany all the way to the 500-metre mark. For a second, I panicked that they might actually beat us, but I quickly turned that thought around. "No way," I thought. "We have worked too hard for this."

As we picked up our pace in the last 250 metres, we easily soared past Germany, not only finishing in first place but also setting a new world record! Our time was 03:21. Great Britain's heat came down next, and GB came in first with a time of 03:23. They could be beaten! At that moment, I realized we had a shot at the gold medal.

Jeff warned us that if we were not careful, this performance could be the worst thing that could have happened. In Beijing, the Canadian wheelchair basketball team finally beat the USA in the semi-finals. This victory was such a huge accomplishment for them that they lost focus on the final and ended up losing to Australia, a team they had never lost a game to. He was worried that this world record could do the same to us, so we put that celebration behind us and stayed focused on the work ahead.

The morning of the final, we arrived at the course as soon as it opened and went for an eight-kilometre paddle just to keep us moving. I laughed as I thought about those days in Montreal, when eight kilometres would have been a tough workout for me. Now I was doing it just to stay loose for a race.

We went back to the hotel to eat and rest up until the final. As I got ready to leave again, I put on my Canada unisuit. I could now wear a unisuit proudly; I looked like an athlete, and I was fit. I thought about the time Marnie McBean had spoken to us at a camp in Tennessee. She told us that we don't earn a medal on race day; we earn it on each and every day that we push ourselves that little bit farther. I definitely felt I had earned a place on the podium. While earlier in the week I had been hoping for silver, now I wanted nothing less than gold. I had never felt so confident and focused before a race. I was completely prepared, ready for anything, and ready to react. Bring it on!

CHAPTER 20

Laura's voice comes through calm and clear. "Okay, we have got this. I *know* we can do it, but we have to do it together, and we have to move now. We're going to stretch and send this boat together for five here... That's it, it's working!" I can hear the excitement building in her voice.

"We're coming into the last 300. We're going to hang on that oar and swing out." She emphasizes the word "swing" to help us feel the rhythm. "Swing through Great Britain. Okay, it's time to sprint... In two we're going up: that's one... that's two..." Her voice is as loud as it can go and starting to go hoarse. "Now! Through the water! More! In two — going up again."

I can hear how excited she is. I know that our efforts are succeeding.

"Vicky! Do it for your kids!"

I haven't used that as a motivator for a while — this last year I've been proving something to myself — but as I hear it now, I feel a fire inside me and I dig deep and feel strength.

"We're walking on them, Canada! Oh yeah! Going up again—"

I knew it! I can't believe we are doing this. I have to hold on and focus. Where is that line?

"Power on the legs… Here! Everything! Five more strokes, right through the line…"

Her voice cracks as she exhales the word "down," telling us we can stop.

We collapse over our oars, and we're all gasping for breath. I feel like I'm either going to die or vomit, one of the two. No one can talk for a while. I'm pretty sure we did it, but I'm not certain…

I hear Laura slap the water behind us and shout, "YES!"

Then I hear Meghan screaming behind me and Tony yelling. We did it! I think I'm in shock.

I throw my arm up in the air and scream. Immediately, I think of Eamonn and the kids and all we've been through. I pat my heart as a sign for them. I hope they're able to see this somehow. I think to myself, "We did it!"

I sit there in the dark, the goggles still in place, listening to the cheers around us, hearing the congratulations from other boats. I'm still struggling to breathe normally. I pat David on the back and laugh, exclaiming, "We did it!"

He is still bent over trying to recover and doesn't reply, but he reaches back and gives my hand a squeeze.

As thrilled as I am, I'm still in agony. I can't believe that hurt so much. I still feel like I'm going to die, but we are being called to the podium, so we have to row over there. We do our best to pull the boat over to the dock. I'm feeling nauseated, and when we get to the dock I have to crawl out of the boat. I take the goggles off, but I can't see straight. The sun is bright, and I don't think my brain is working at all. Laura takes my arm and guides me to some chairs where we all sit so we can breathe for a few minutes.

By the time we are called up for the victory ceremony, I feel a little more in control of my body. I know the families and supporters in the crowd are going crazy even though I can't see them. I smile blankly into the crowd and wave. Meghan tells me her mom is crying.

A gorgeous smell wafts over us, and I realize we are being presented with flowers. They are such a vibrant yellow that I can see them, too. We are also being presented with gifts from a local Maori artist; a hand-carved jade necklace has been designed for all the gold-medal winners. Meghan tells me it is carved in the shape of their war canoe paddle. I am speechless. I have learned during this trip how important greenstone necklaces are to the Maori people, and I am honoured to be a recipient.

World champions

Now the medals are being presented, and my name echoes through the stands — "Victoria Nolan!" — as my medal is placed over my head. Instinctively I pick up the medallion and look at it. Even though I can't see what is engraved on it, it feels beautiful in my hand. I am overwhelmed.

As we stand there on the podium, I remember everything: the blisters on my hands in Montreal; losing to the US at the Henley; rowing away from the victory ceremony in Beijing; and those days at home with my babies when I thought I had no hope of success in my future.

Then it's time for the moment I dreamed of years before: the Canadian flag is raised and our national anthem plays. We sing "O Canada" as loudly as we can, grinning from ear to ear. Our eyes well up with tears of pride, and we can't stop smiling. I'm standing there so full of pride, thinking about my family. I am thinking about my future. I write these last lines surrounded by darkness, but I've never been so full of light.

EPILOGUE

The thrill of victory did not end there. As we left the podium, I could hear our High Performance Director running at full speed toward us. He threw his arms around Meghan in a giant bear hug and swung her around. Then he hugged me, saying, "Victoria, you are an amazing lady!" He moved on to hug the rest of the crew. I was thrilled to have made him proud. We were the first team to win gold under his direction.

The rest of the team had family back in the grandstands, and they went to see them. That was a lonely time for me. Jeff and I waited for the team to return, both of us wishing we had our families there too. Then Eamonn called me on my cellphone. He had watched the race online and screamed so loudly that he had woken up Ceili. He told her that I had won a gold medal, and she screamed and did a little dance before going back to bed.

By far, the biggest high I got from winning was from the story Eamonn told me the next day. Tarabh had arrived at school that morning, walked into his grade-two classroom, and gotten a standing ovation because his mom was a World Champion.

On the way back to the hotel, we saw our training partners from the lightweight double, and they were thrilled for us. They gave us big hugs and seemed genuinely happy for us. Their final was the next day, and they had been training at the gym when our race was televised. They told us that they were on the ergs when they watched, rowing with us, increasing their speed on the machines as we increased ours in the race. Then they cooled down while they watched our medal ceremony. They said they were so inspired by us, that our sprint took a lot of heart. We told them they had inspired us during the race to power through the last 250 metres. I never would have dreamed that we would be the ones inspiring them!

They went on to become World Champions themselves. We won Canada's only two gold medals that year.

On the last day before we left New Zealand, everyone from Team Canada met in the dining hall for a closing meeting. The High Performance Director summed up the event. He began the meeting by saying that Rowing Canada had learned a lot that year. There were some things that had worked really well and some things that had not. One of the things he said worked really well was the Adaptive Program. At that, the room erupted with applause and whistles. It felt amazing. Finally, we had gained everyone's respect.

He stressed that we were the Canadian Team. We were not lightweights versus heavyweights, or men versus women. We were not adaptive versus able-bodied. We were one Canadian Team, and we had to believe it in order to be successful.

That belief felt like an accomplishment in itself. It was a good start in advancing my new goal: changing people's attitudes towards disability.

ACKNOWLEDGEMENTS

I would like to express my gratitude to Jay Teitel, whose guidance and encouragement initiated this endeavour. I am also very grateful for John Rafferty's support in getting my story publicized. I would like to thank Kate Unrau for her advice and assistance in relaying my story in a clear and meaningful way. Thank you to Greg Ioannou and the staff at Iguana Books for your creativity and professionalism. A very big thank you to the Argonaut Rowing Club for giving me the opportunity to do great things. Thank you Meghan, Laura, and Tony — it's been quite a journey. Finally, I wish to thank my parents for their unending support.

Iguana Books

iguanabooks.com

If you enjoyed *Beyond Vision: The Story of a Blind Rower*...
Look for other books coming soon from Iguana Books! Subscribe to
our blog for updates as they happen.

iguanabooks.com/blog/

If you're a writer...
Iguana Books is always looking for great new writers, in every genre.
We produce primarily ebooks, but, as you can see, we do the occasional
print book as well. Visit us at iguanabooks.com to see what Iguana
Books has to offer both emerging and established authors.

iguanabooks.com/publishing-with-iguana/

If you're looking for another good book...
All of Iguana's books are available on our website. We pride ourselves
on making sure that every Iguana book is a great read.

iguanabooks.com/bookstore/

Visit our bookstore today and support your favourite author.

IGUANA

CPSIA information can be obtained at www.ICGtesting.com
Printed in the USA
LVOW10s0126010414

379680LV00034B/2046/P